CATS OF TAIWAN

A PHOTOGRAPHIC JOURNEY
OF TAIWAN'S CAT VILLAGE

GINA KEATLEY
SCOTT KEATLEY

COPYRIGHT © 2019 GINA KEATLEY, SCOTT KEATLEY
ALL RIGHTS RESERVED.
ISBN-13: 9781795421157

Houtong, which translates roughly into Monkey Cave, is a small cat paradise tucked away in the hills of northern Taiwan. A former coal mining town along the Keelung River, cats have been living among the permanent population since the late-1800s. Originally, the cats were brought in to take care of the mouse problem that was causing health issues among the populace. However, in the 1990s the mine fell into disuse and the population declined quickly. With the disappearance of the people and industry there was a decrease in the mouse population, but the cats remained. A dedicated group of volunteers, who go by the name "Monkey Cat Friends Club" (translated), make frequent visits to the cats bringing everything from medical care to food. Over 200 cats are thriving in this tiny town, each with their own personality and habits.

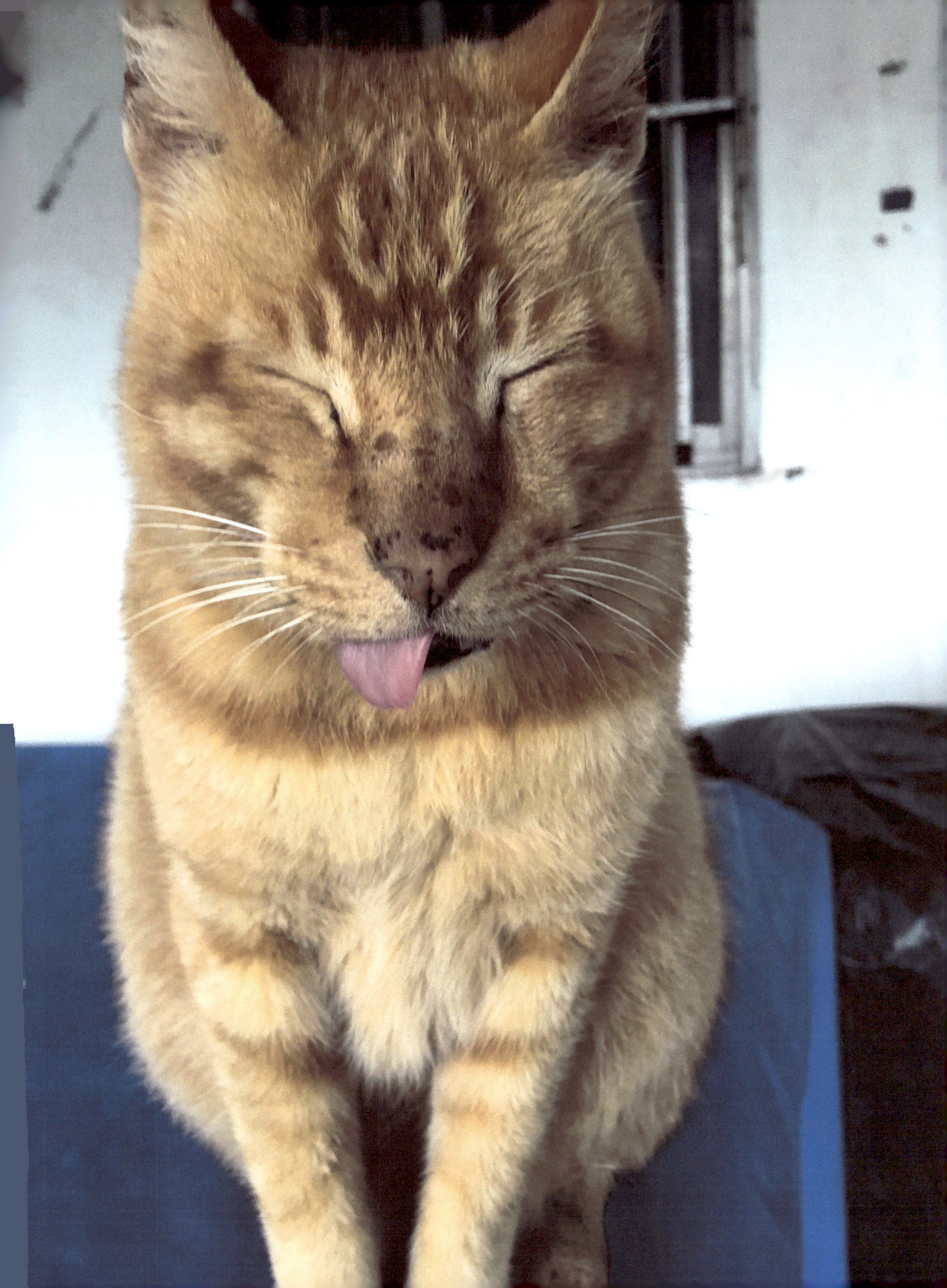

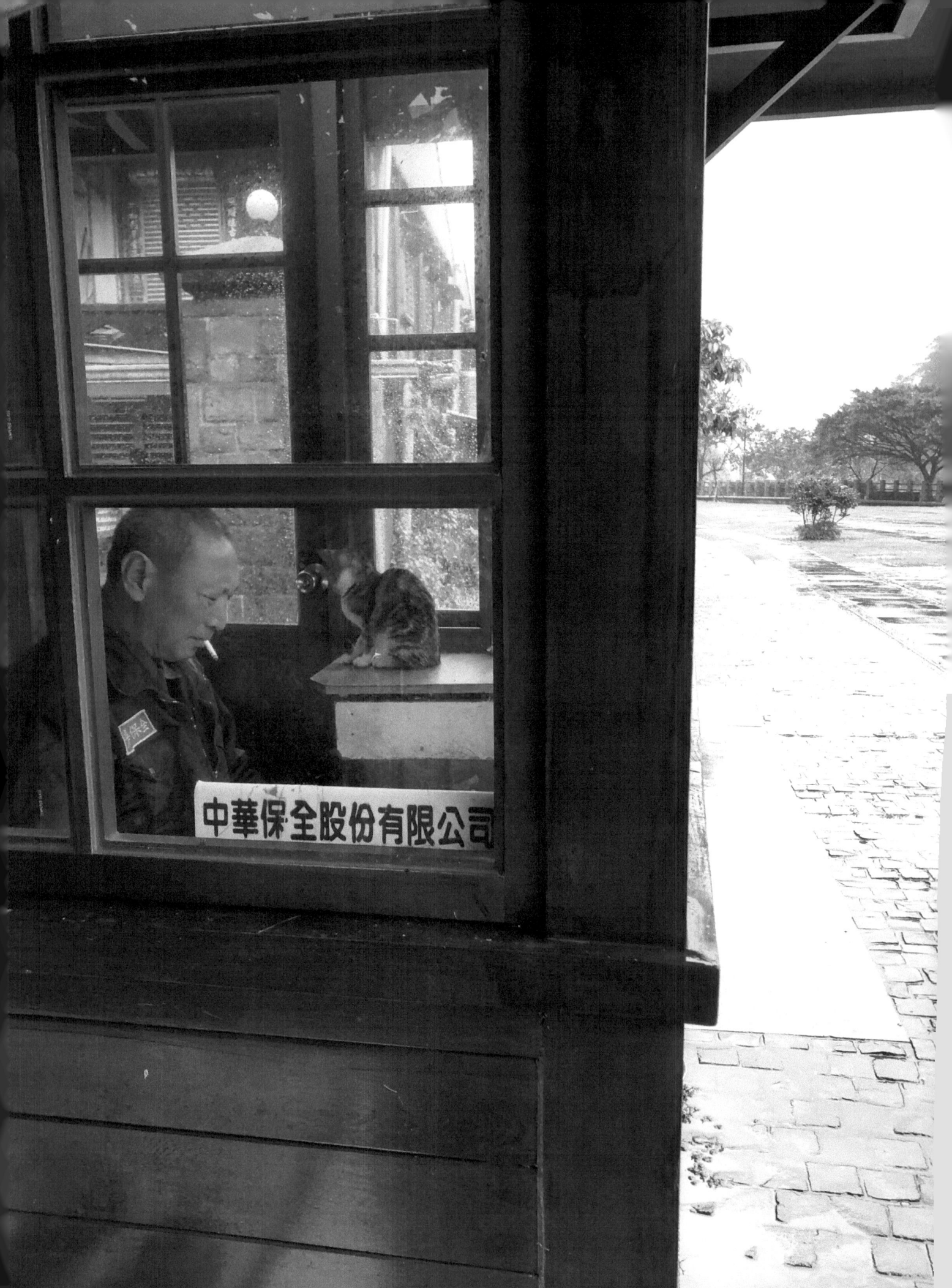

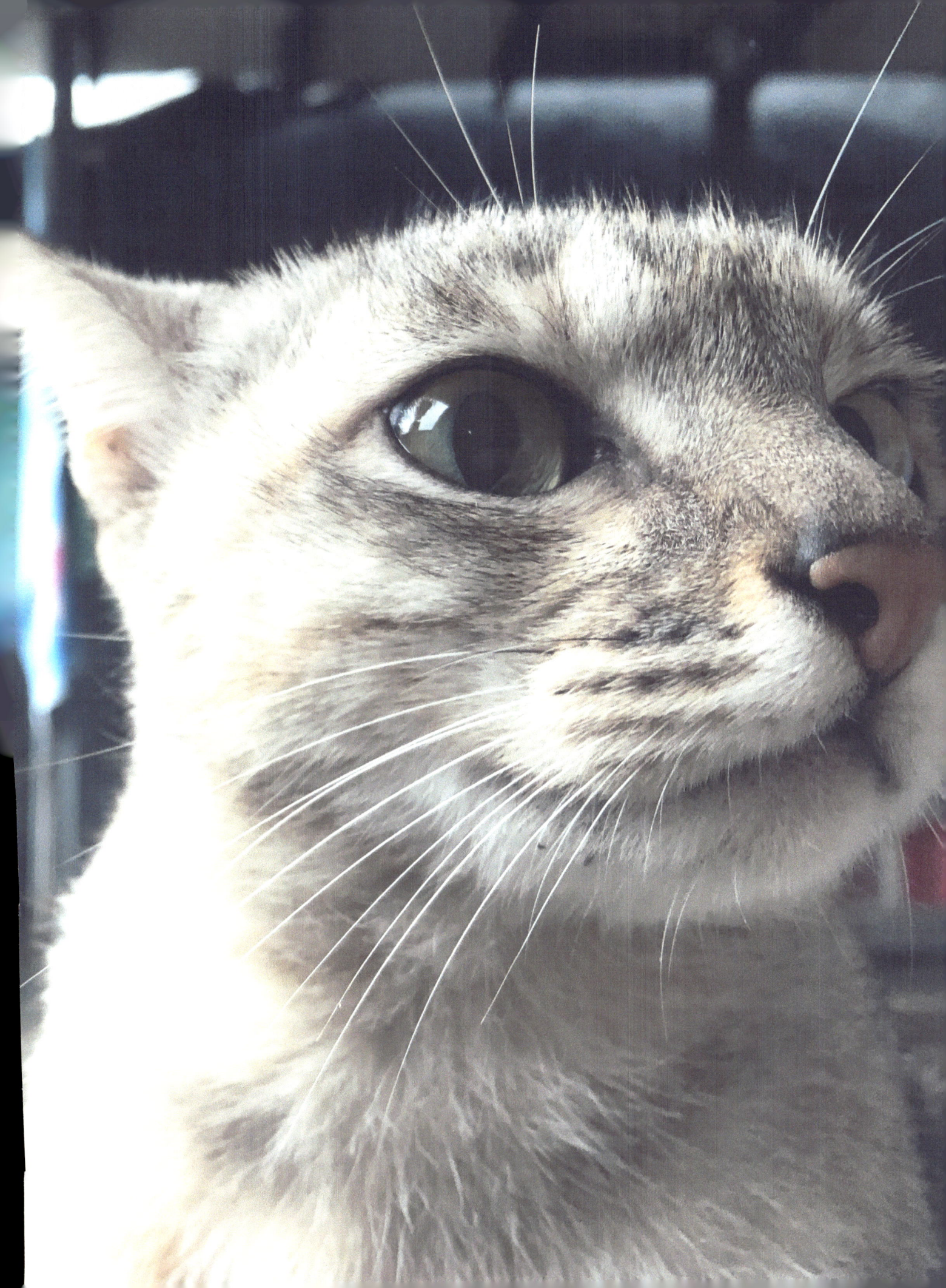

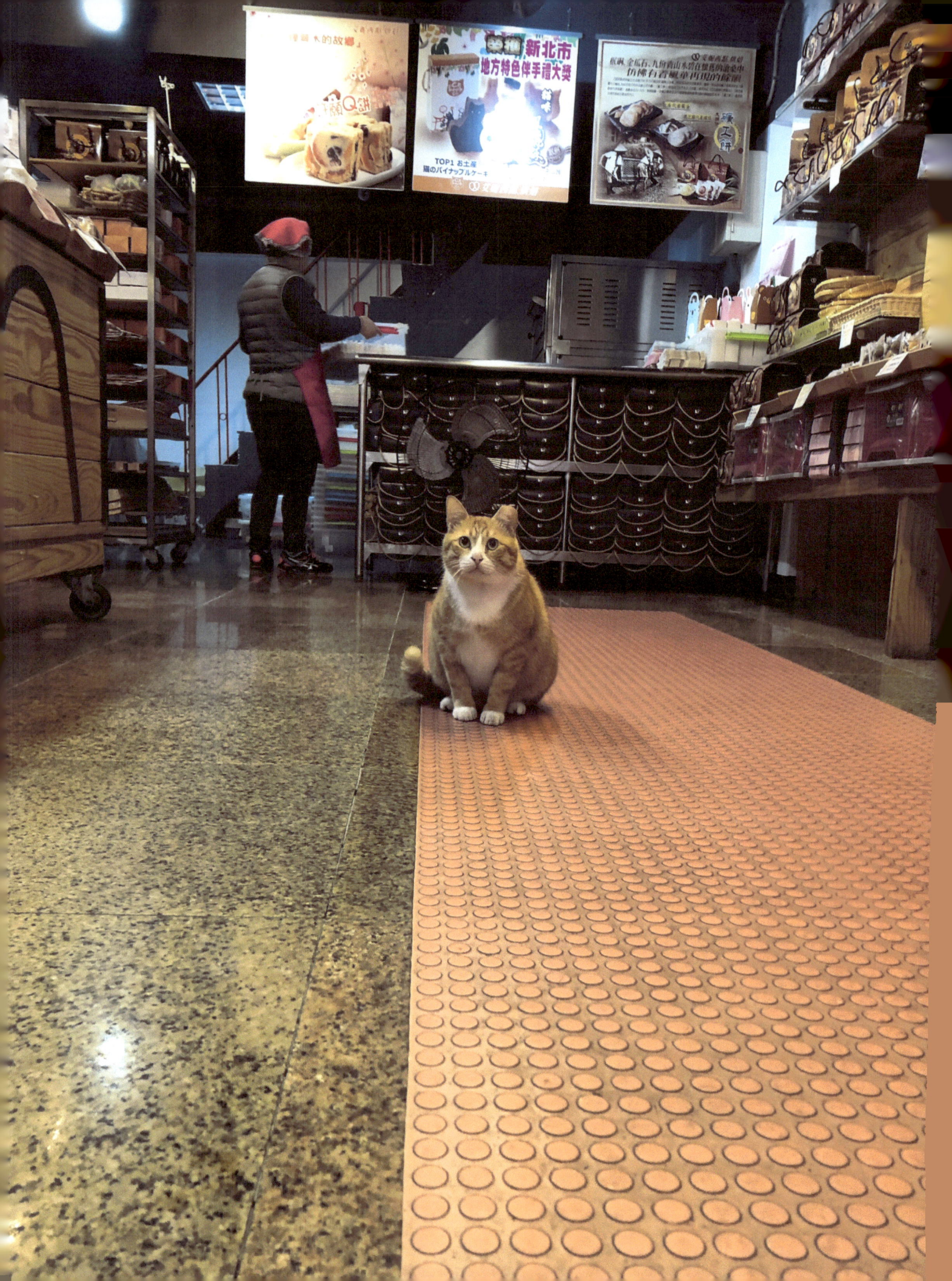

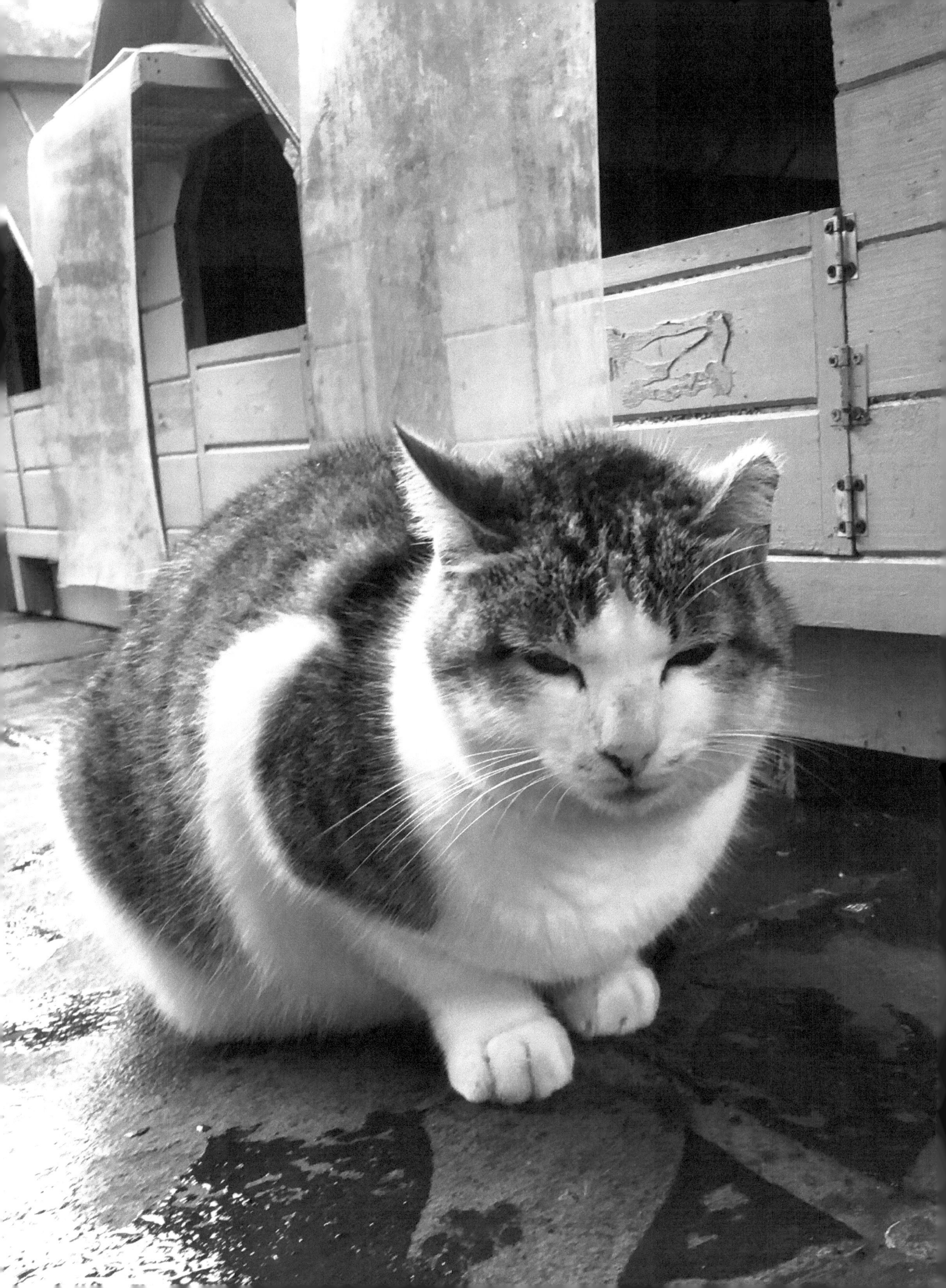

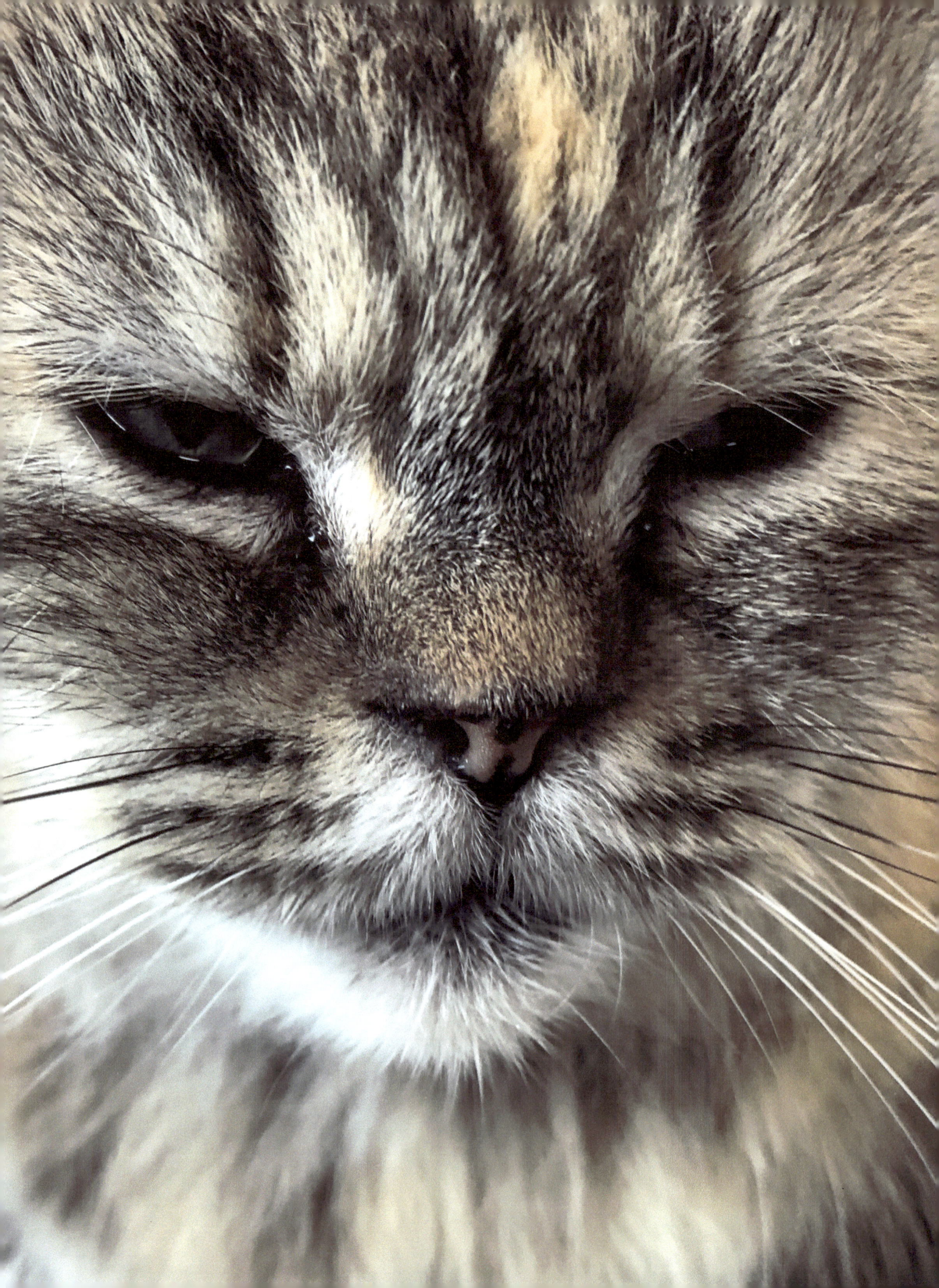

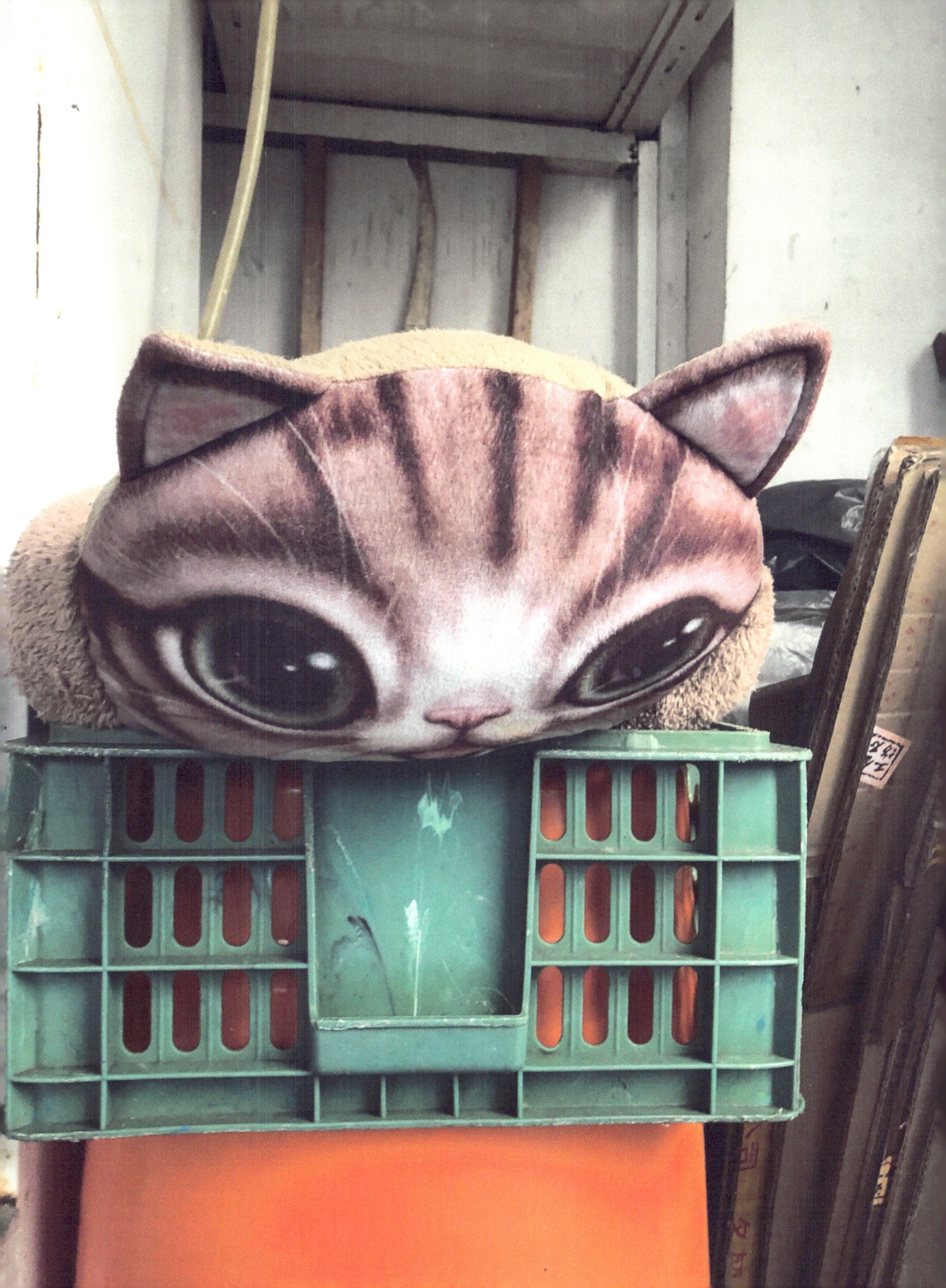

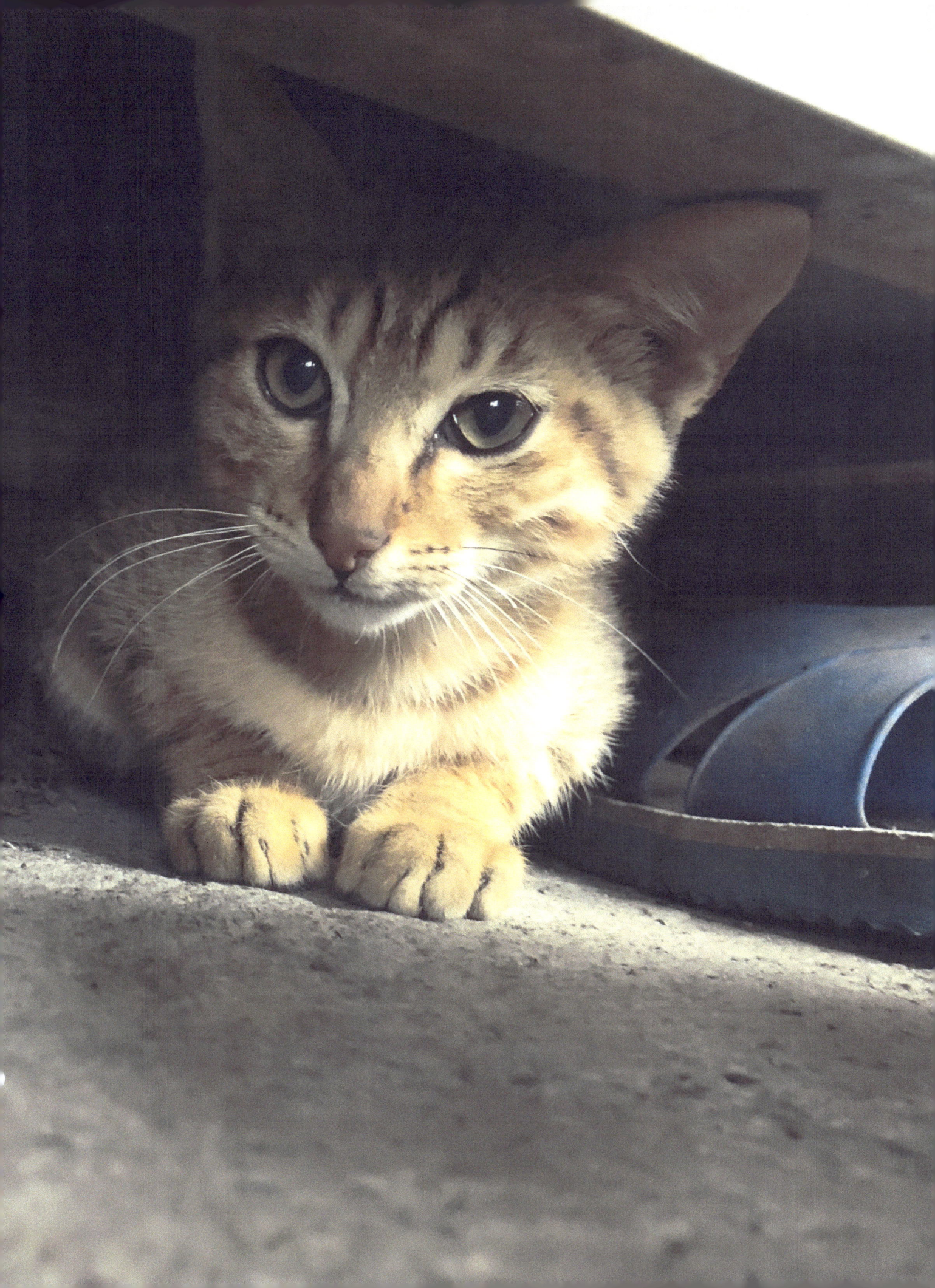

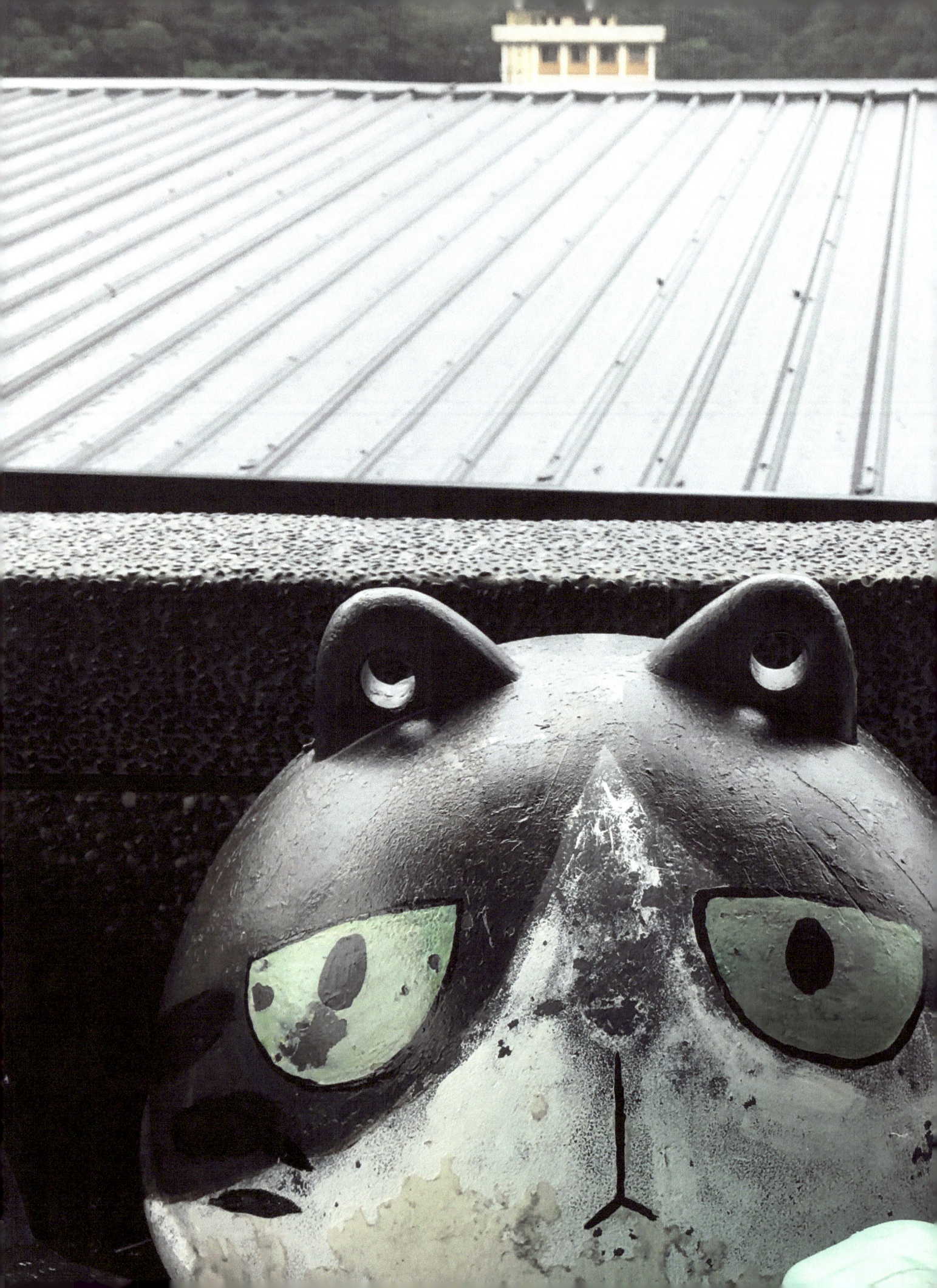

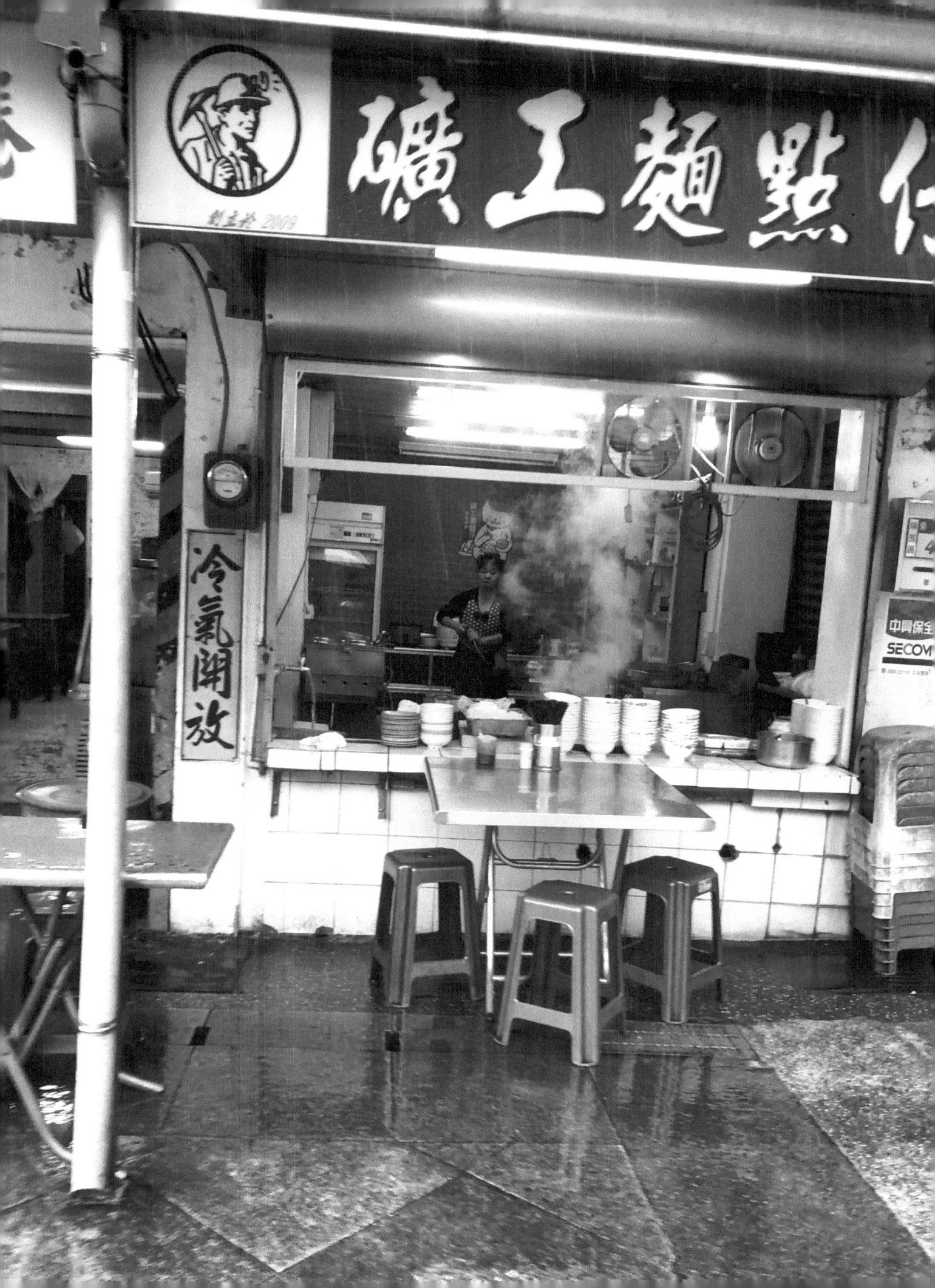

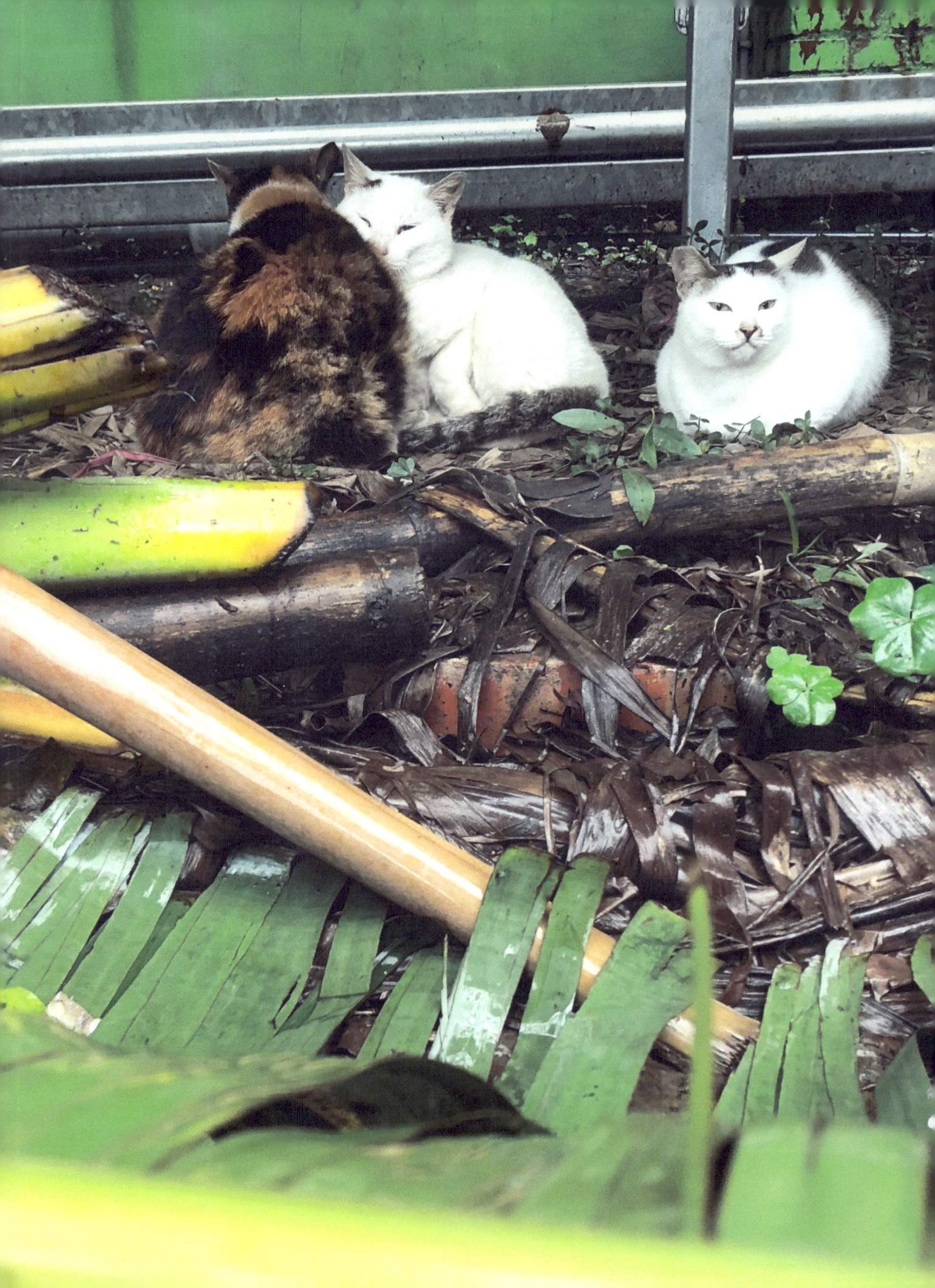

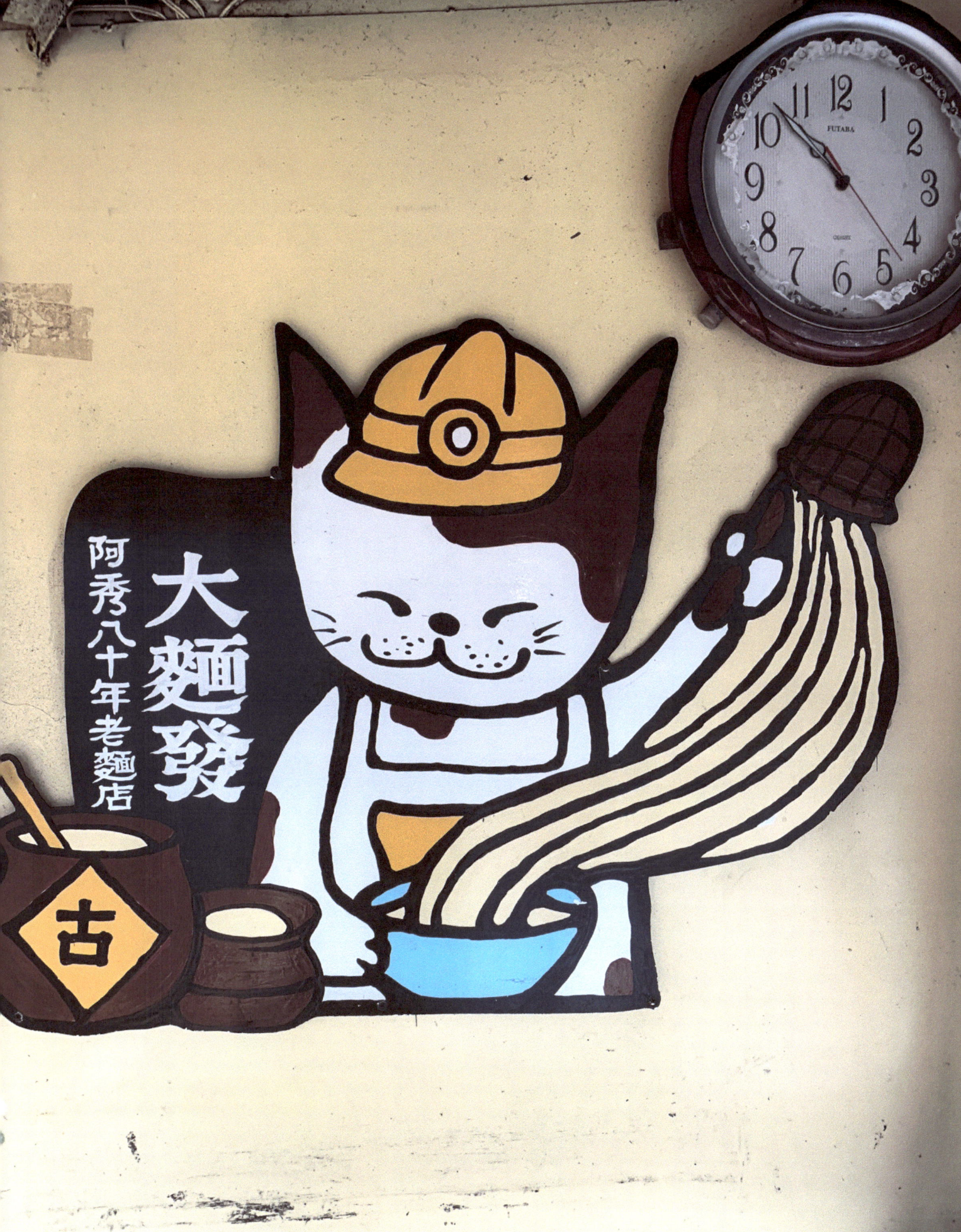

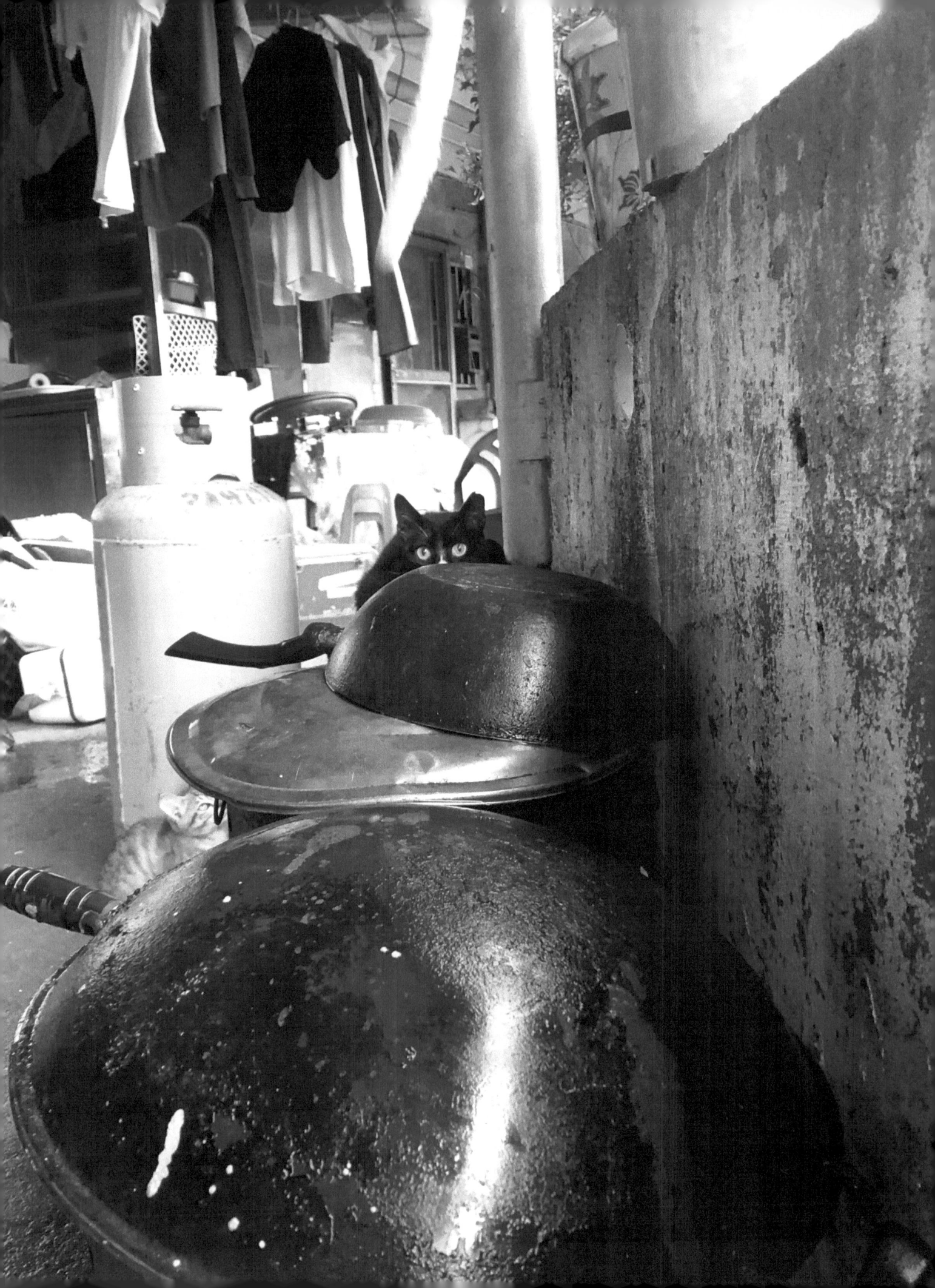

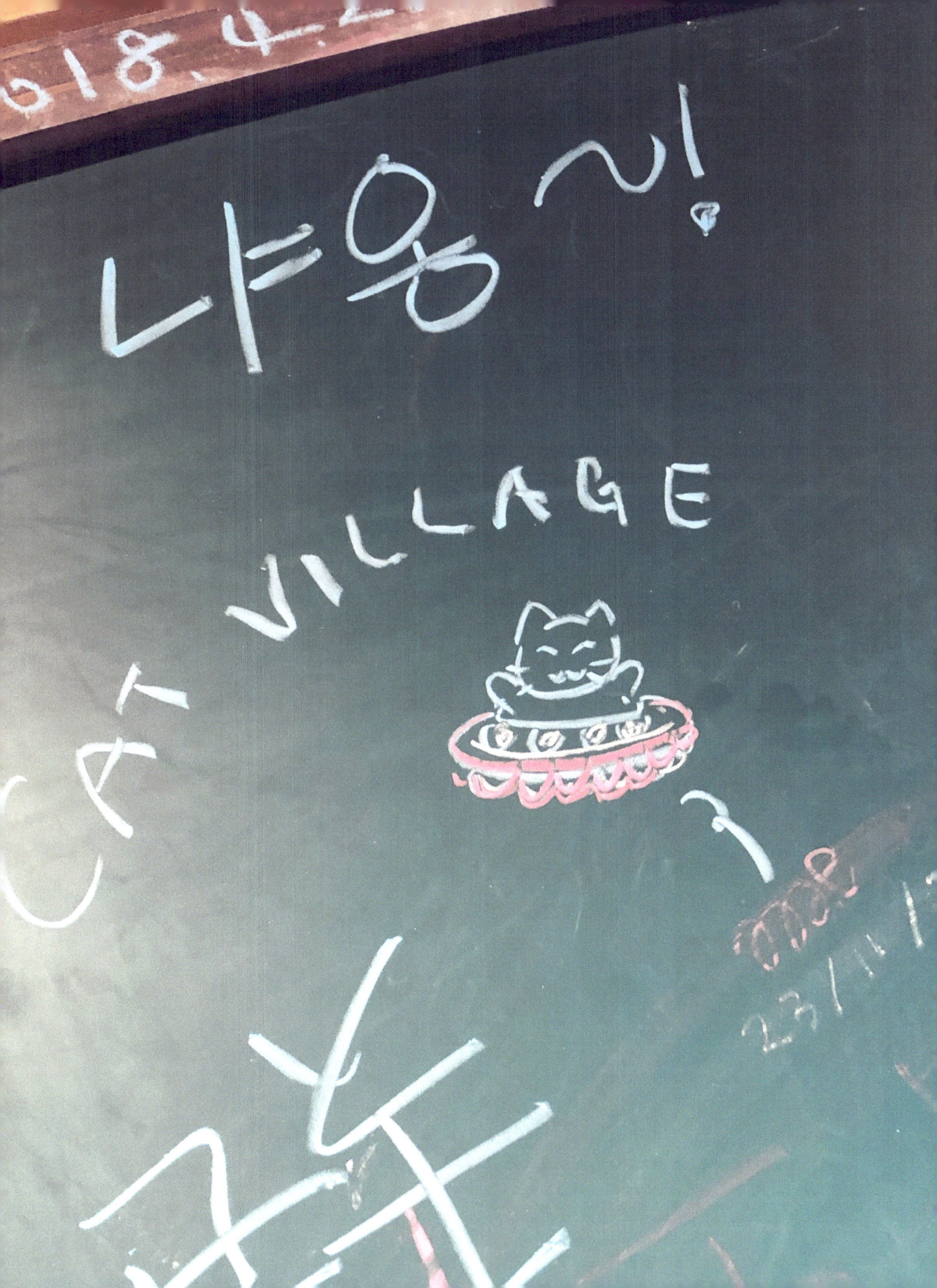

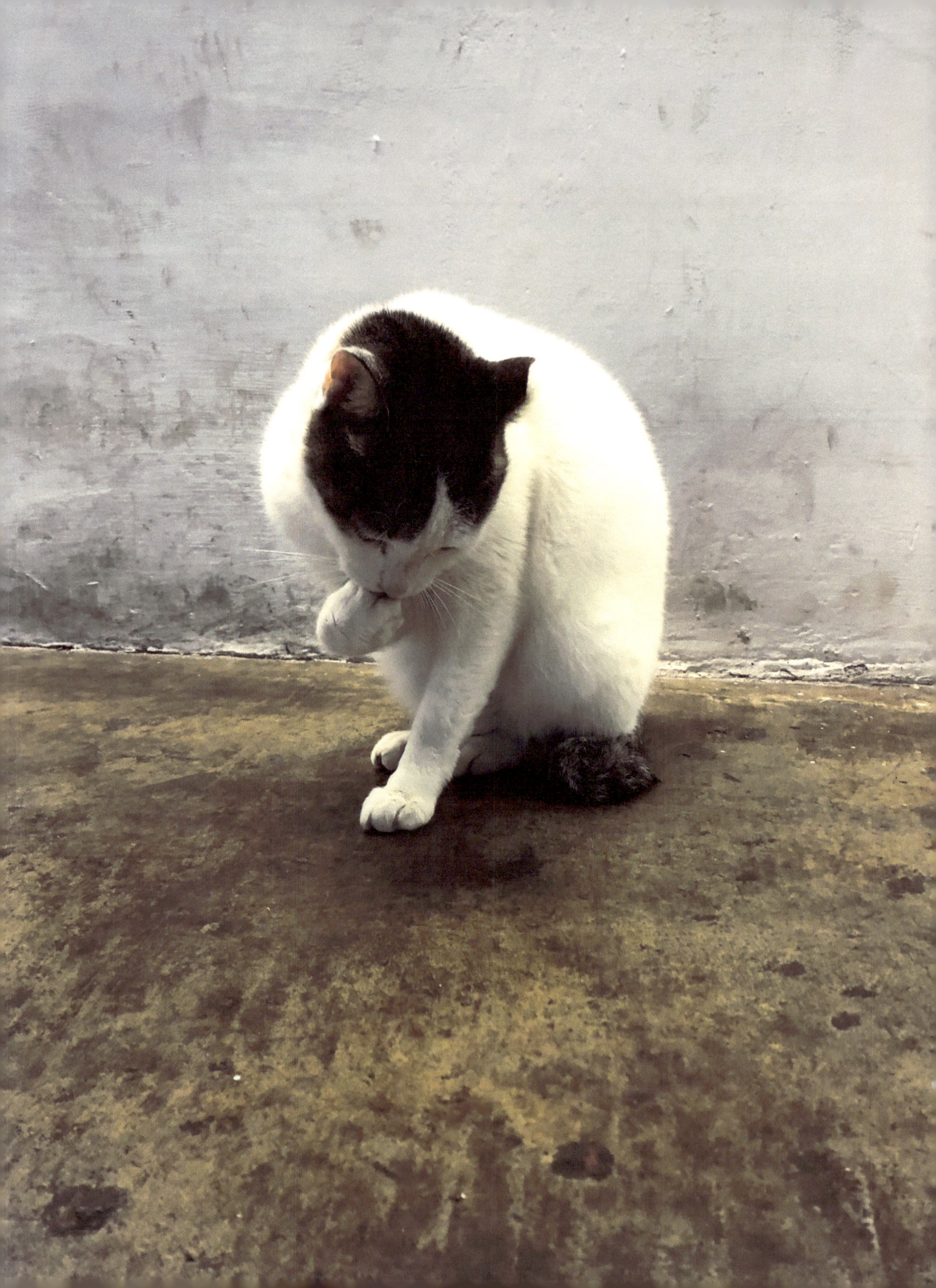

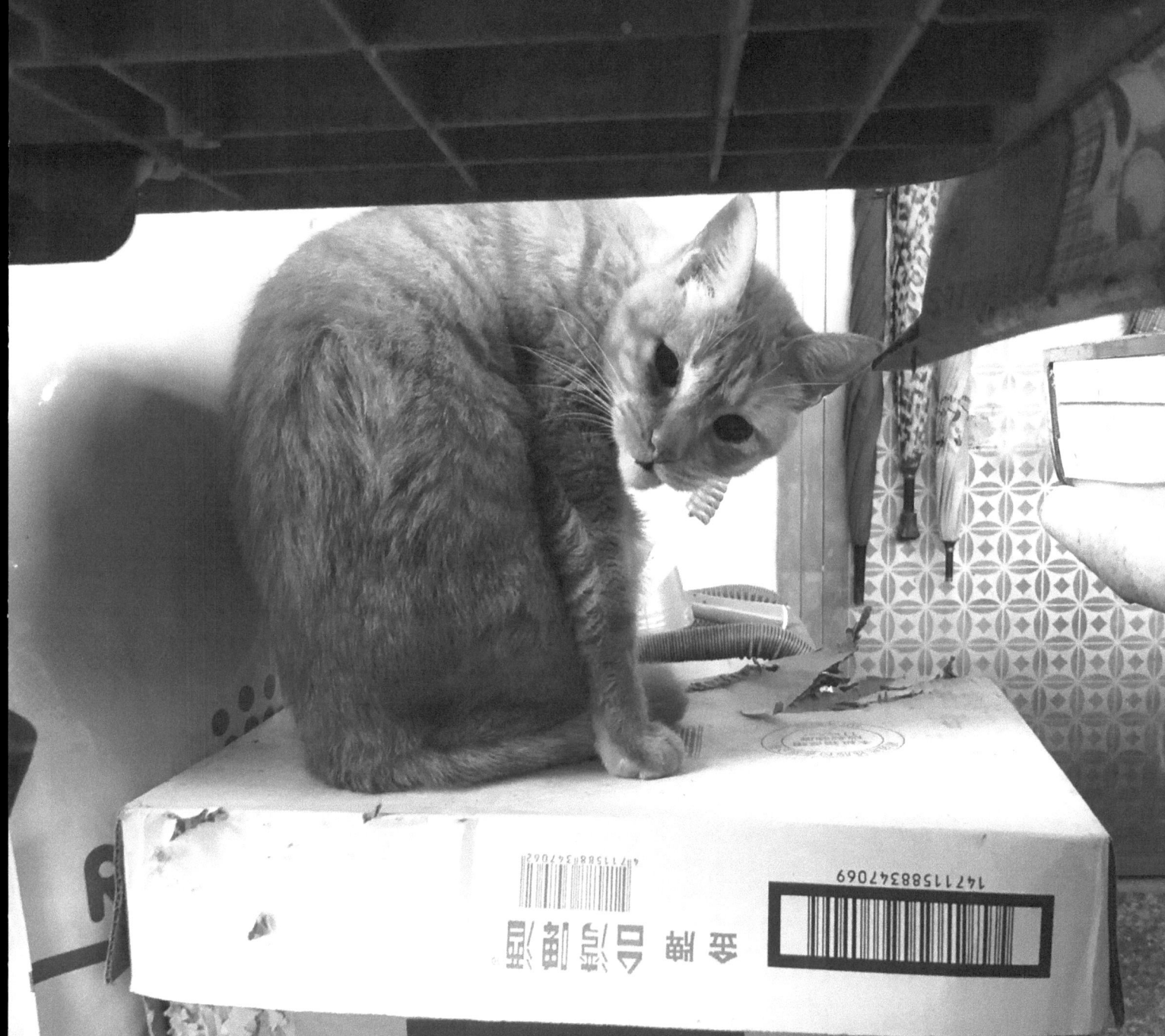

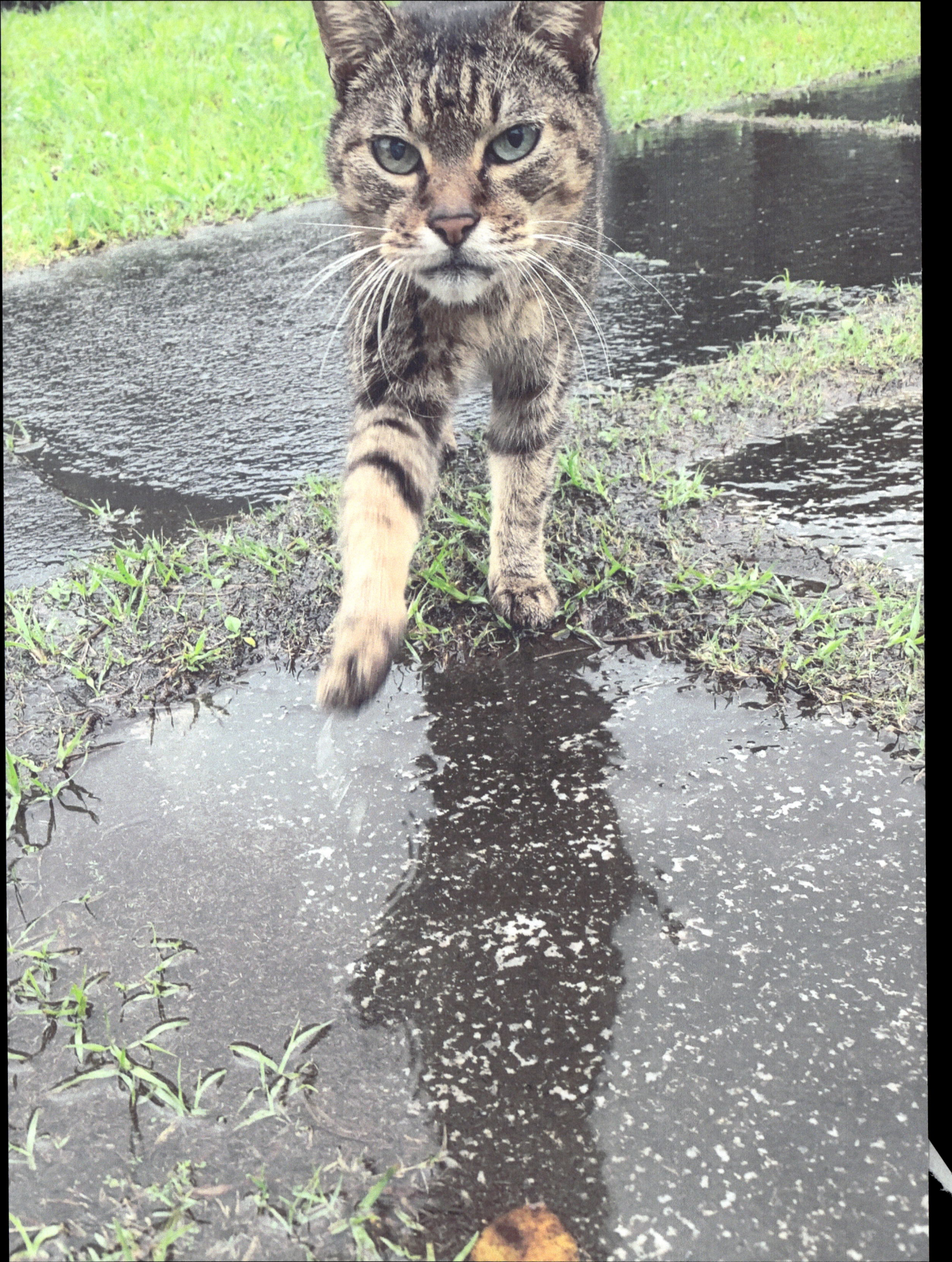

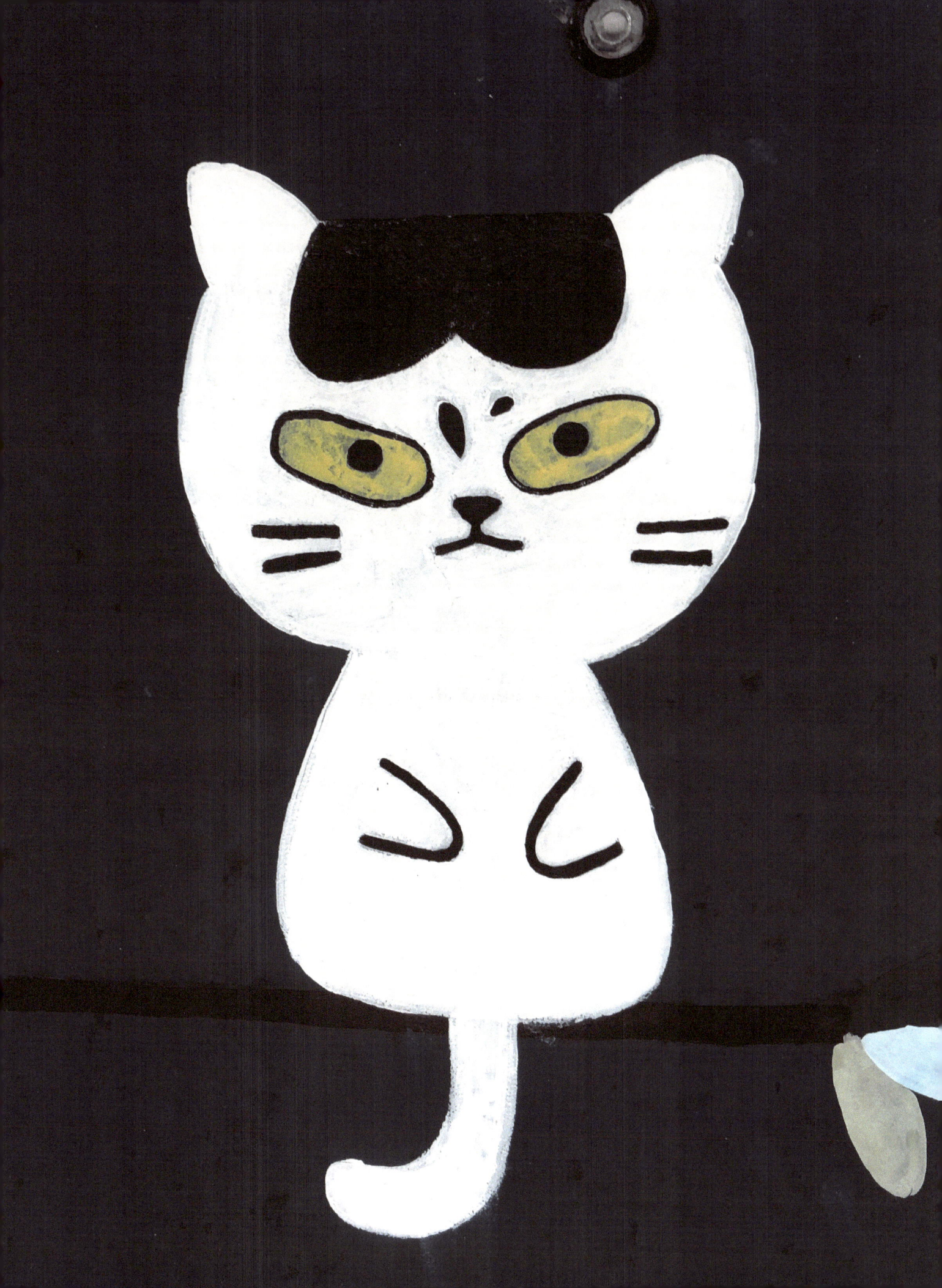

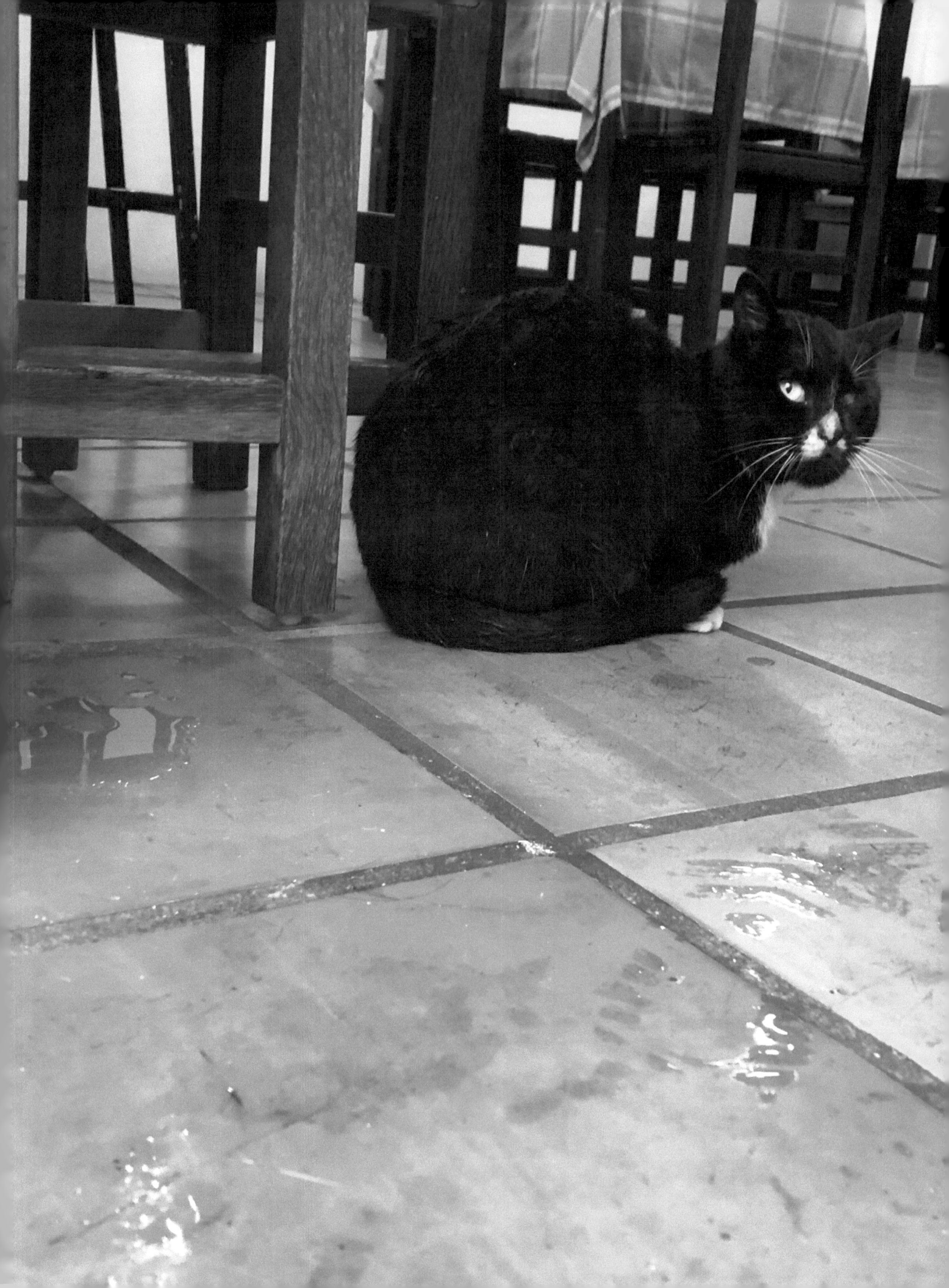

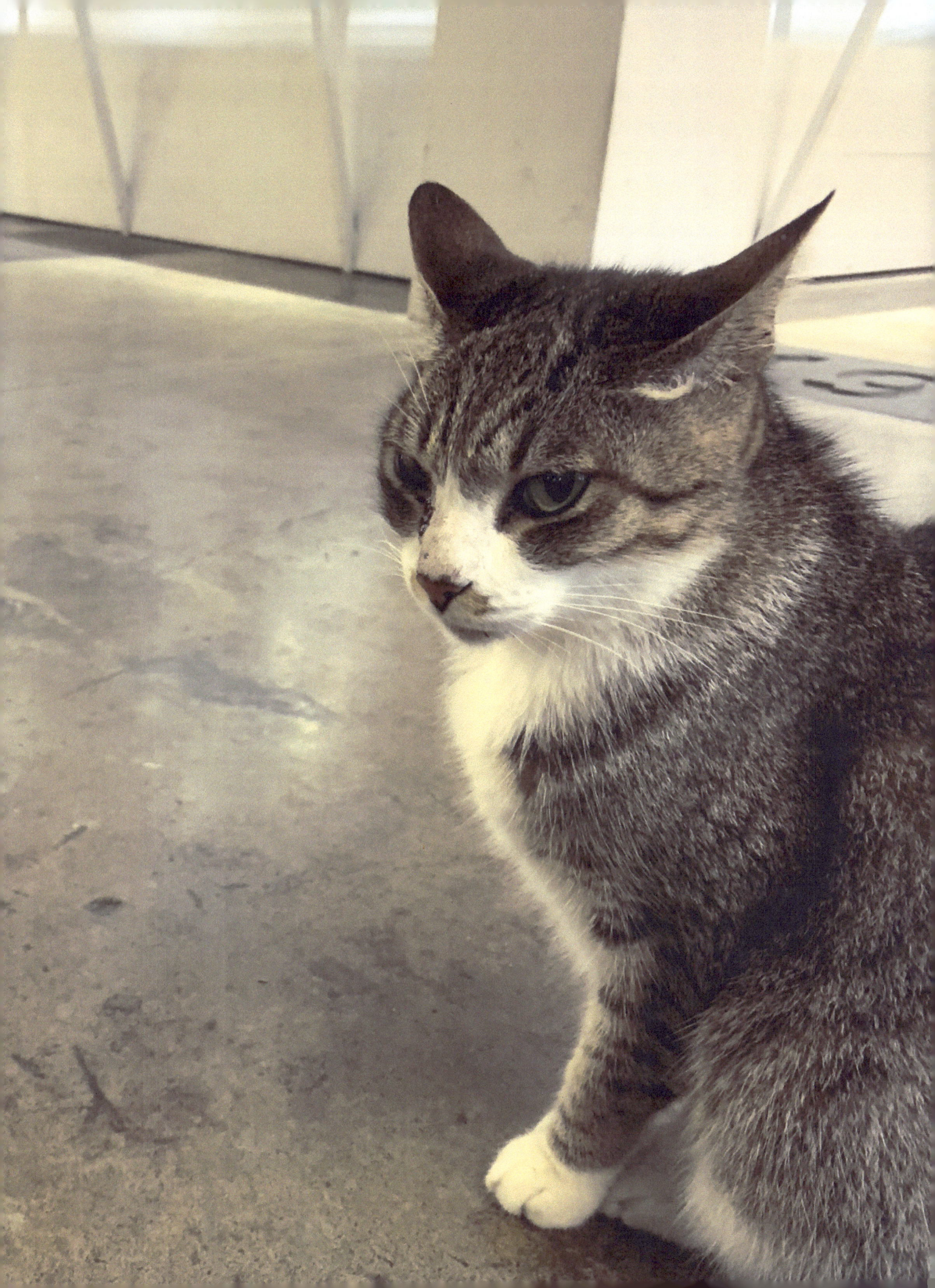

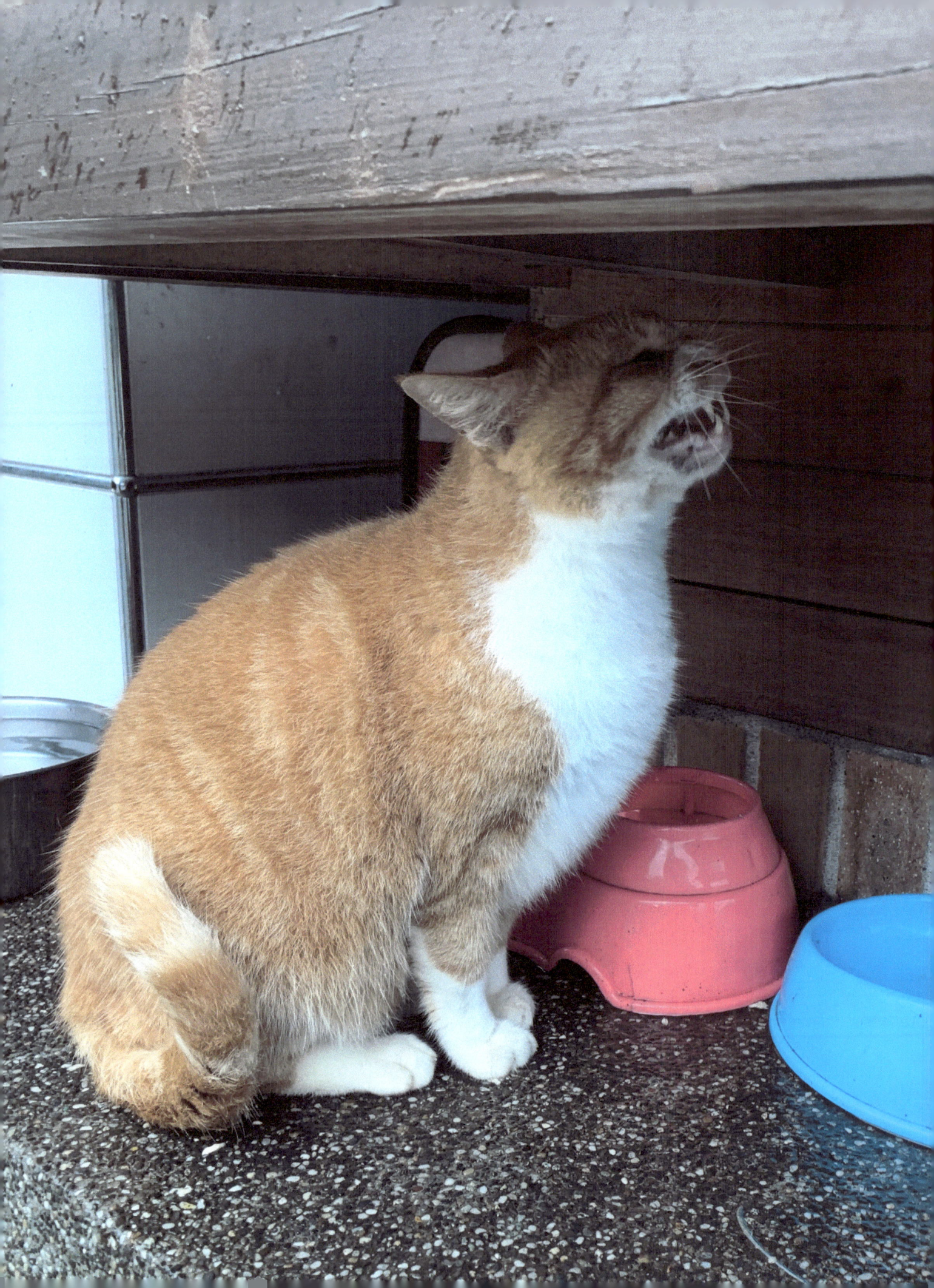

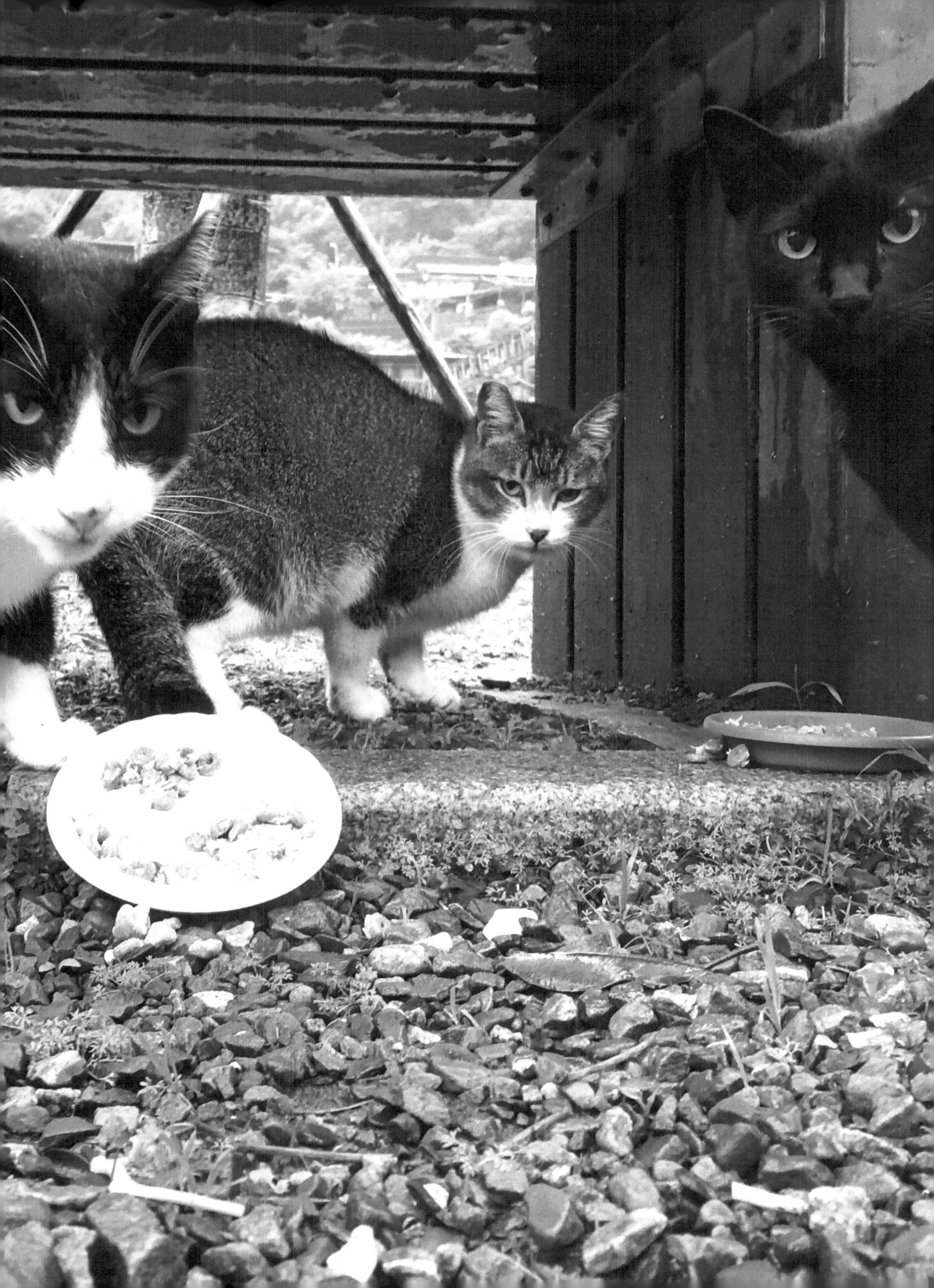

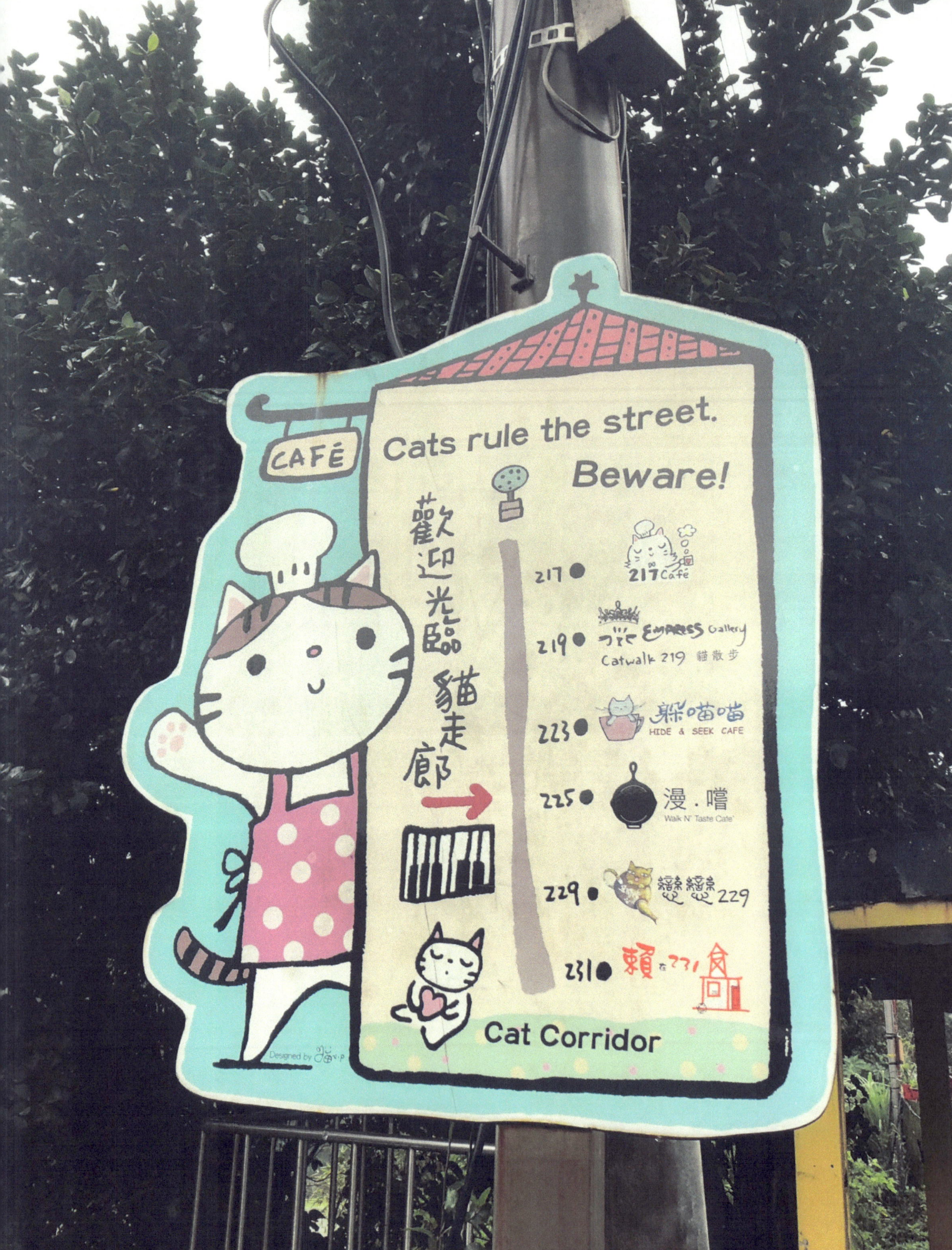

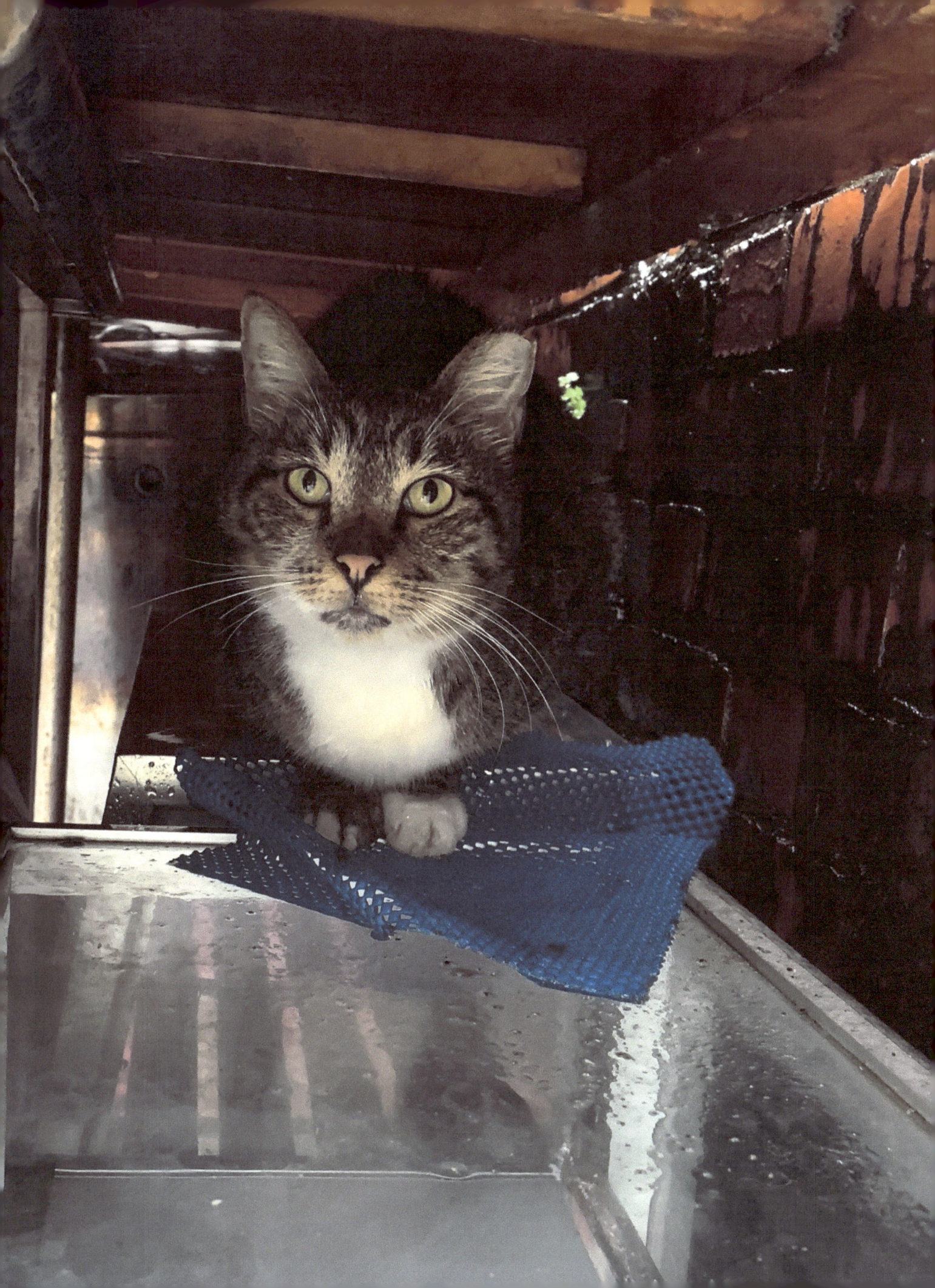

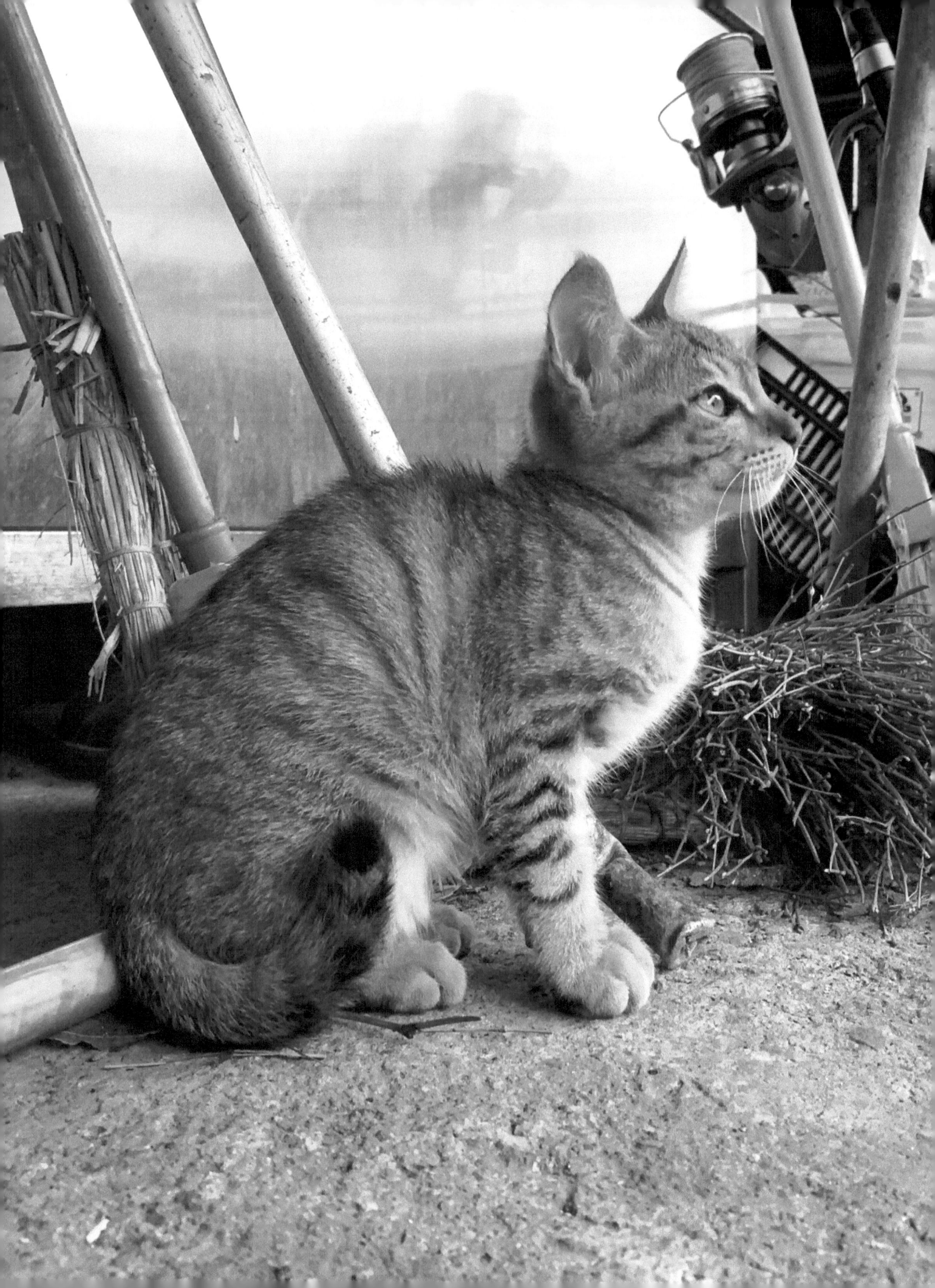

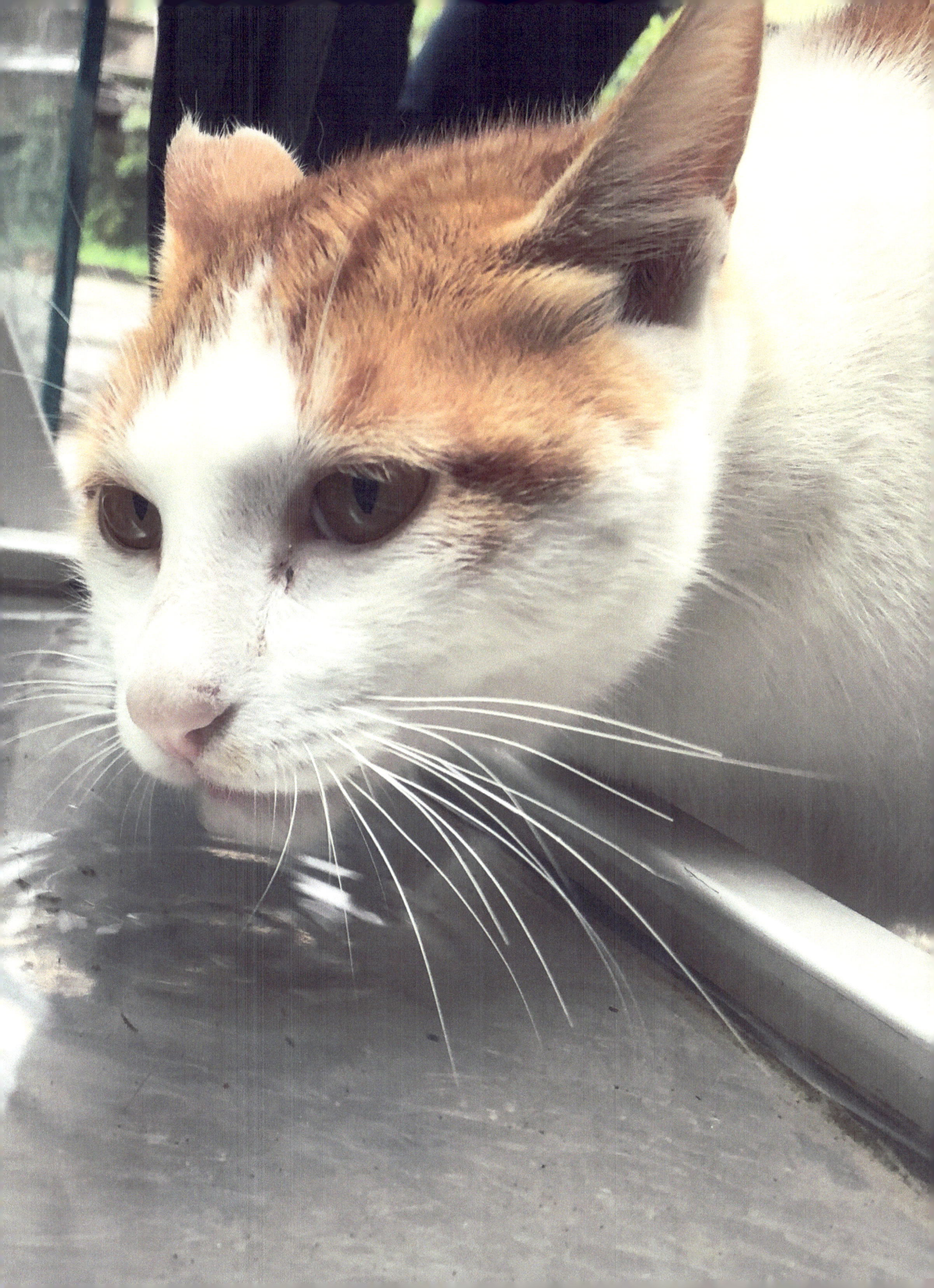

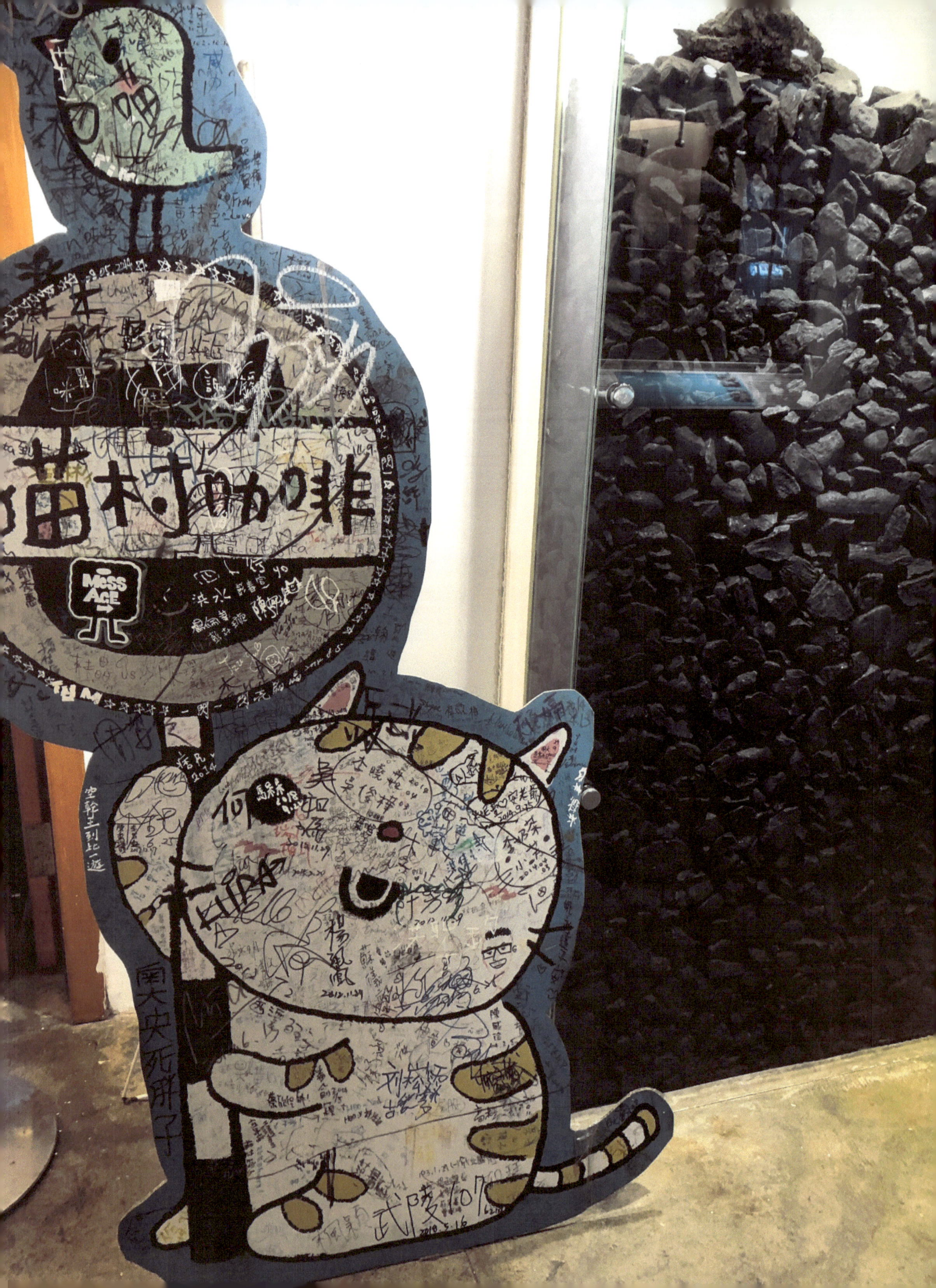

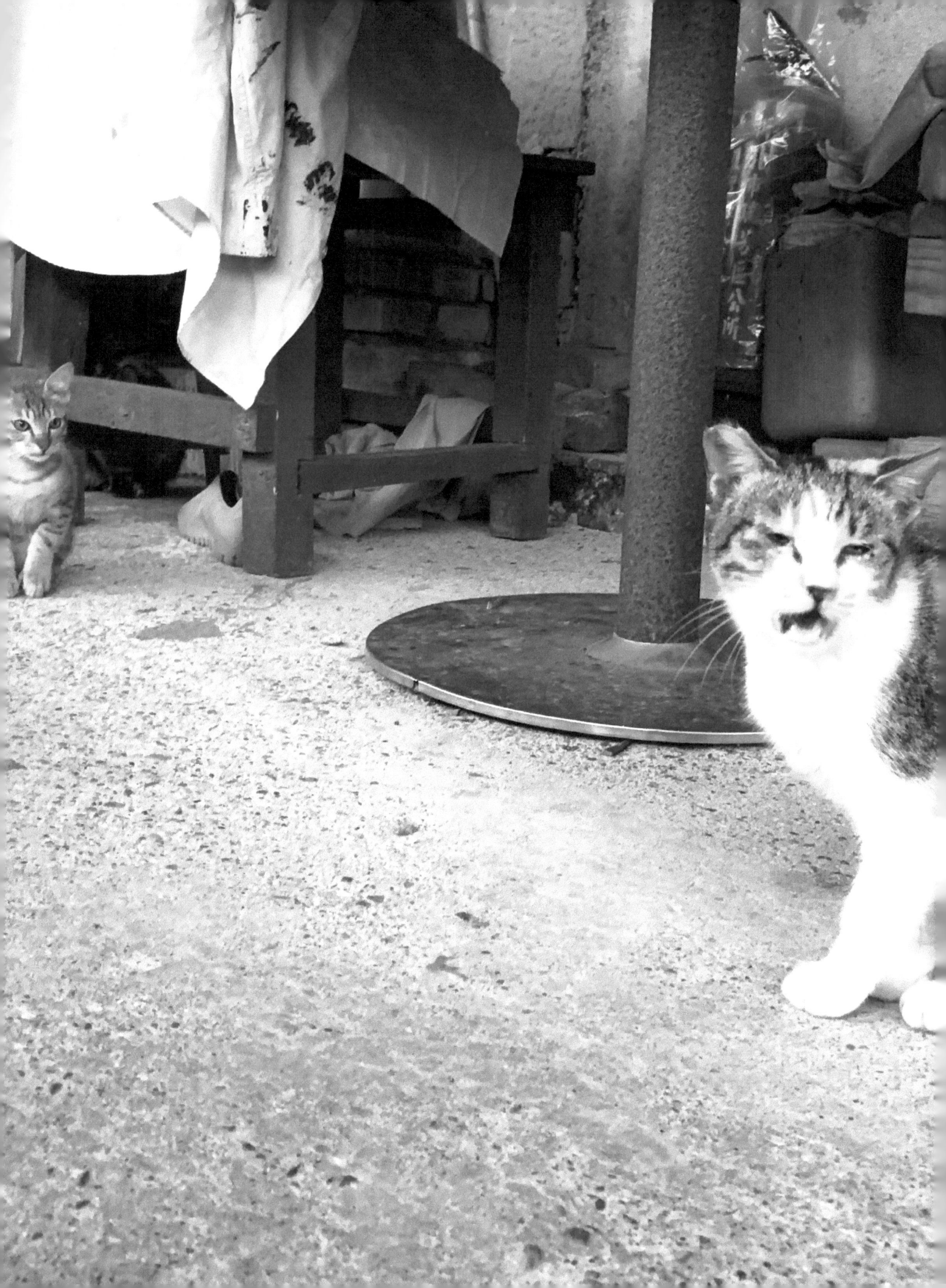

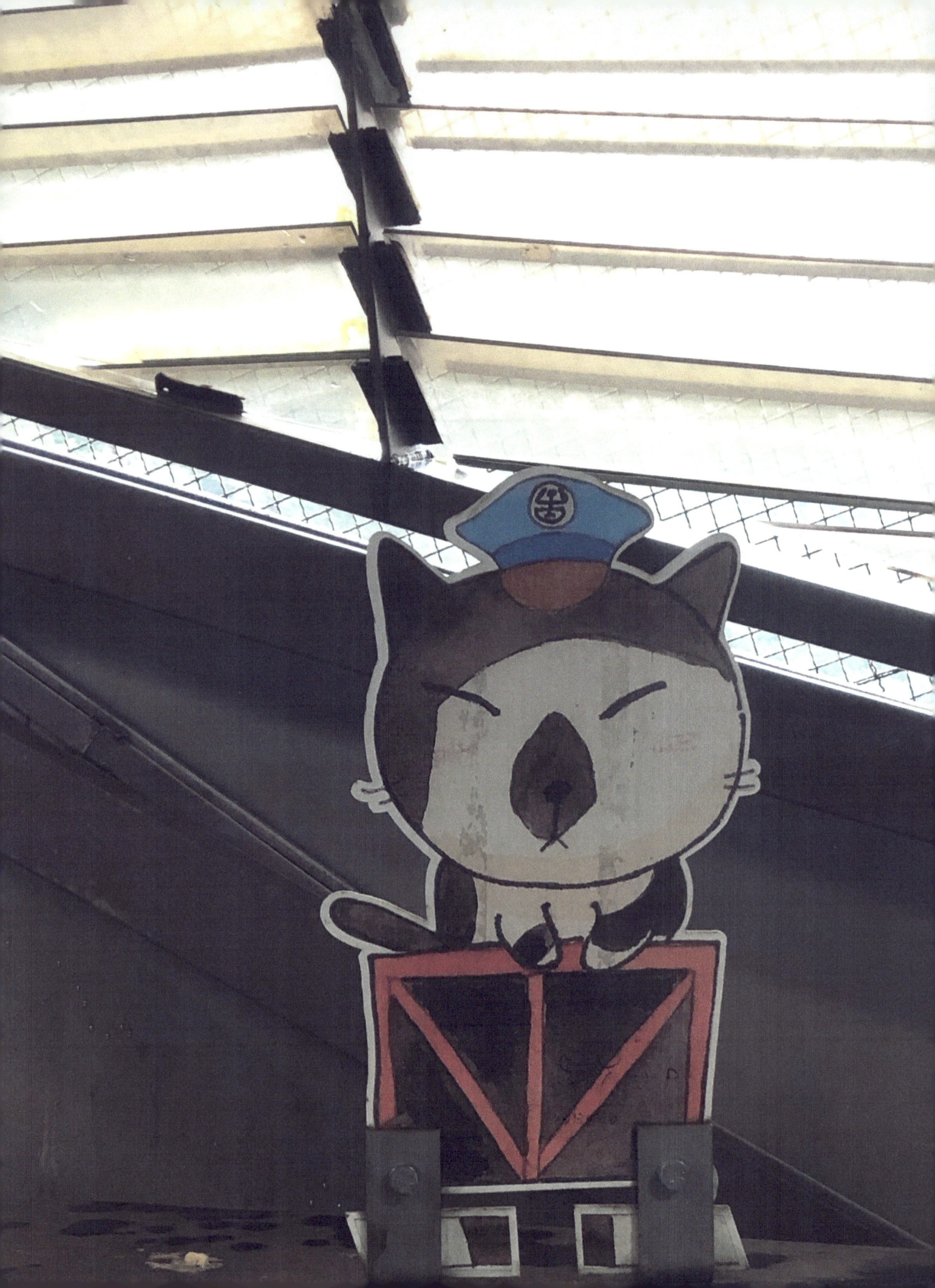

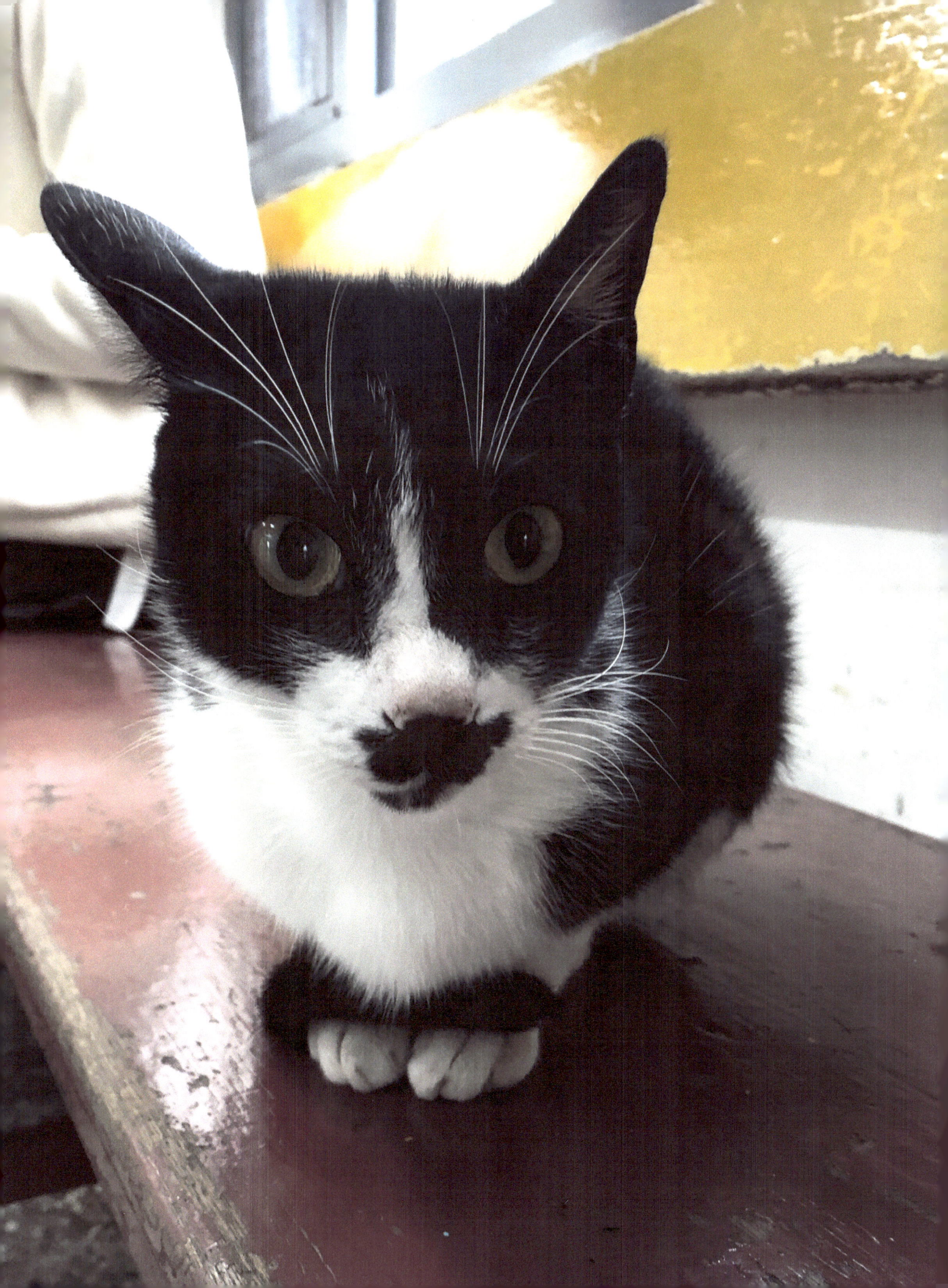

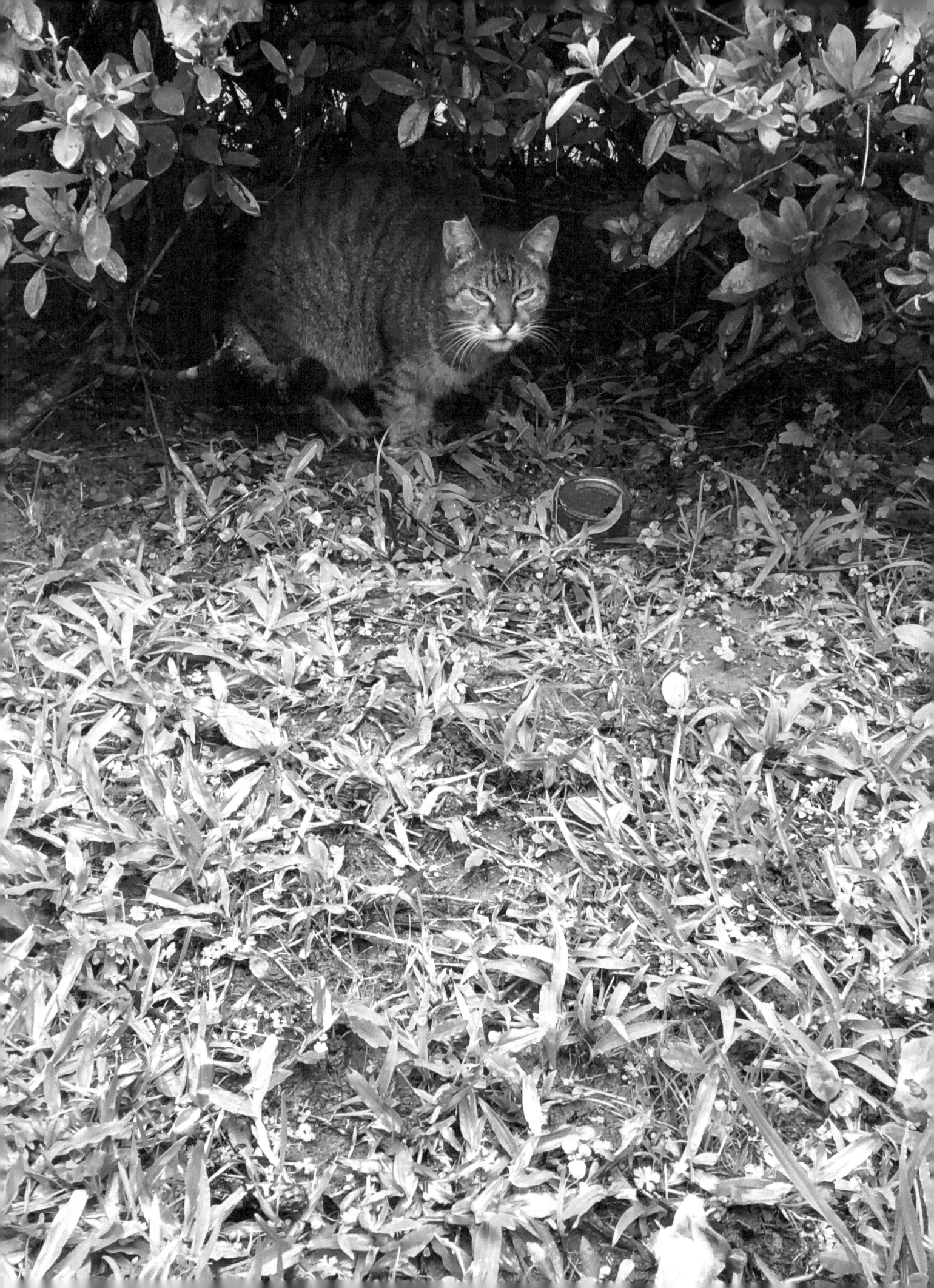

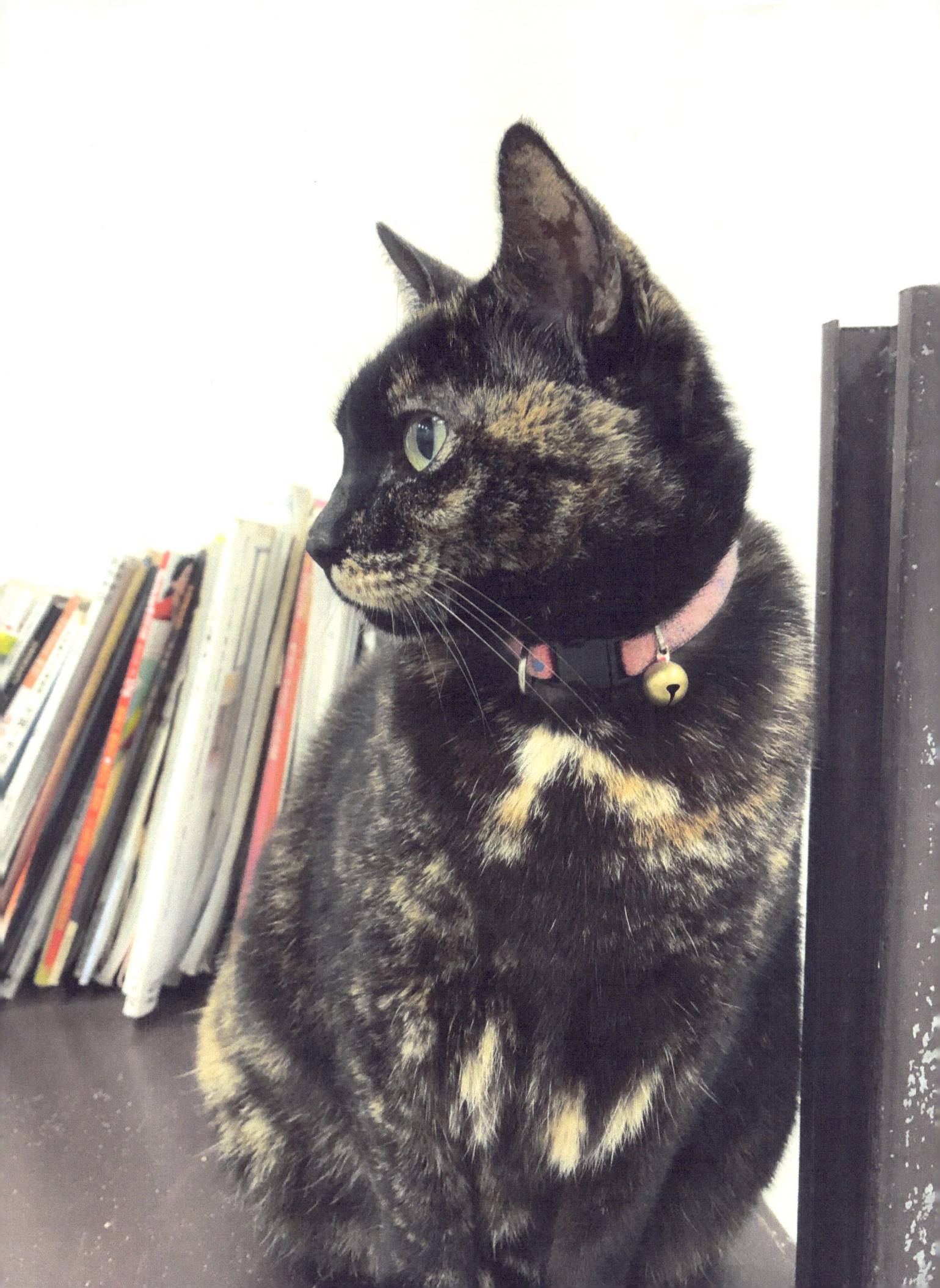

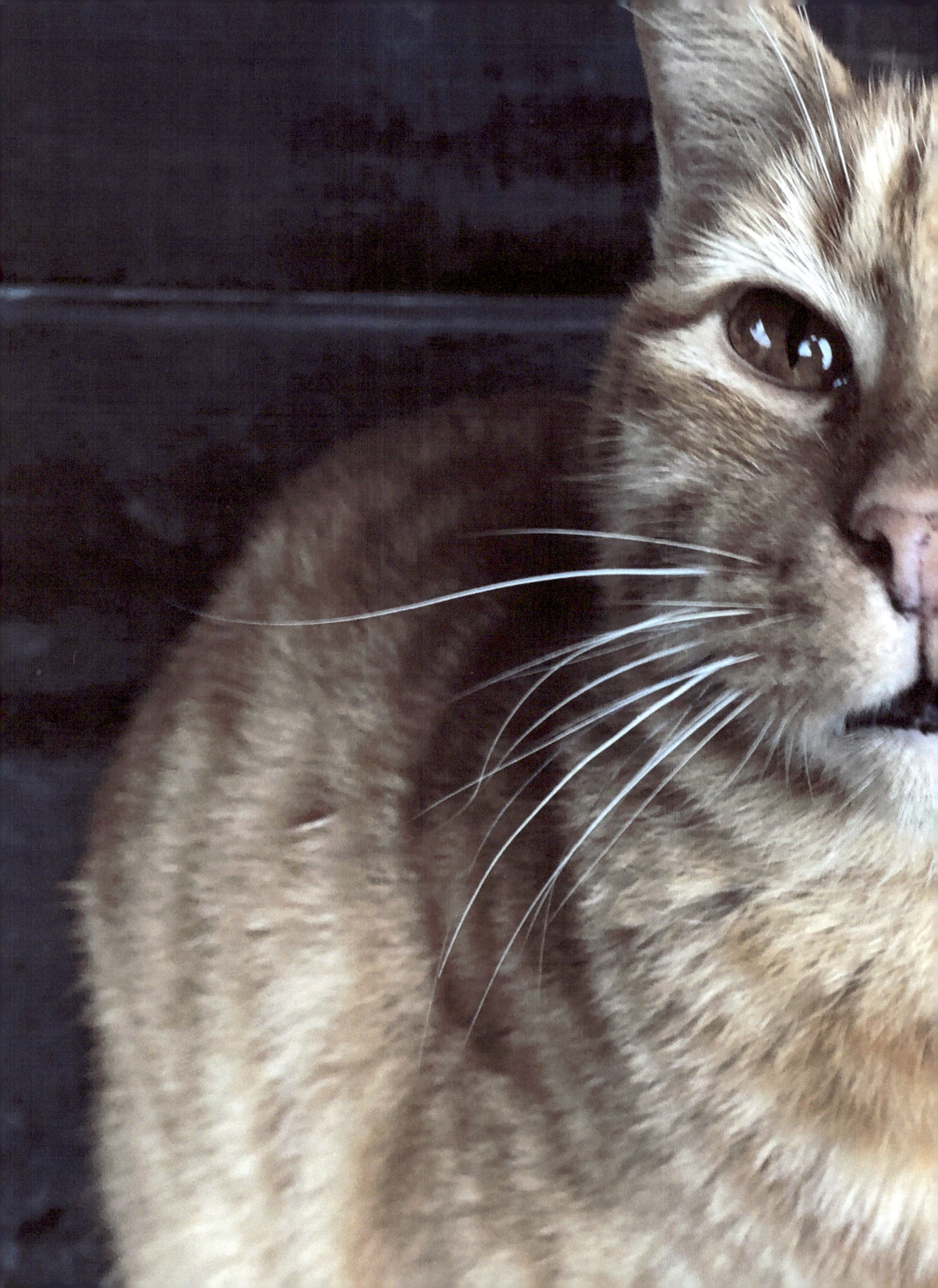

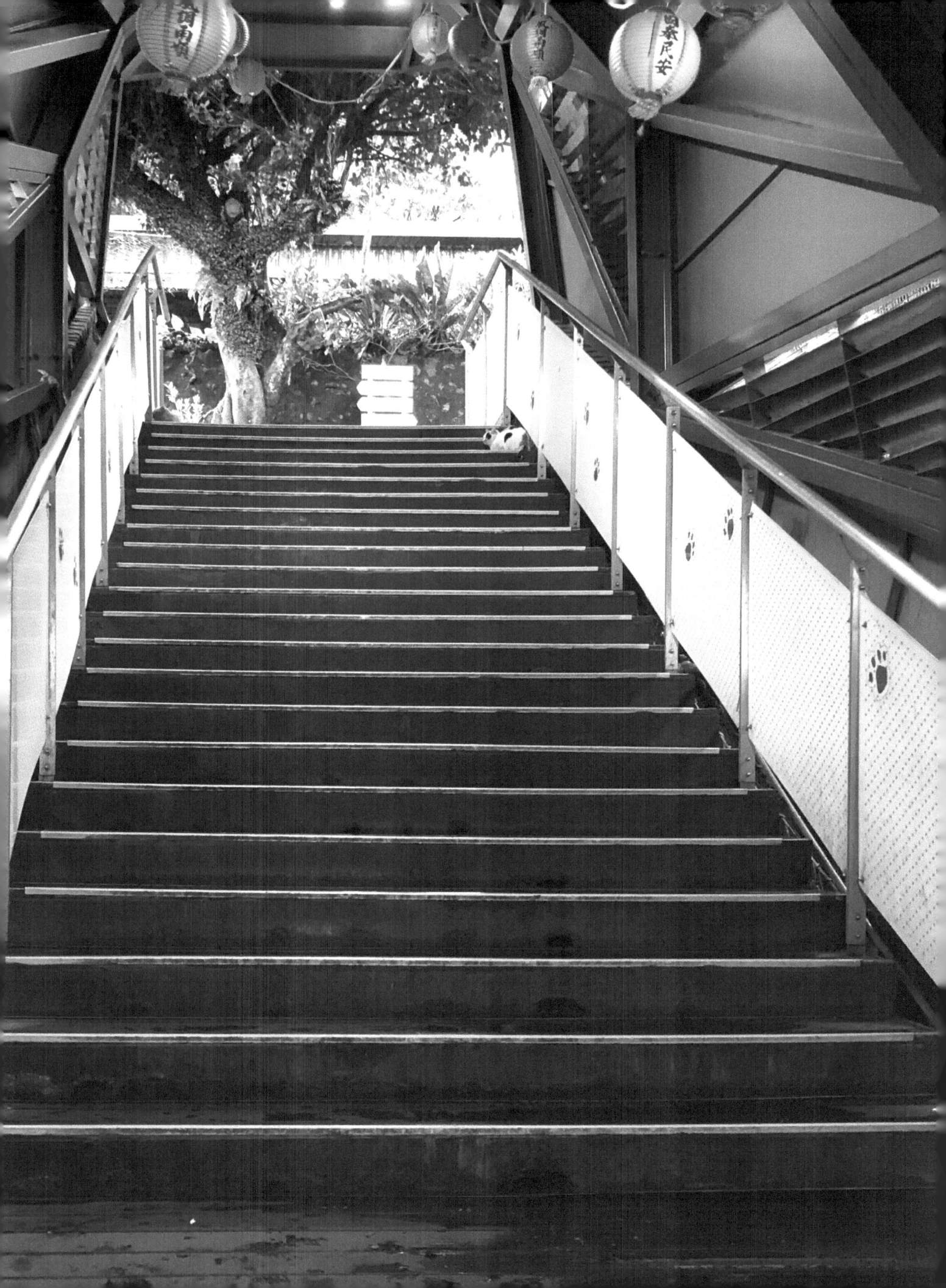

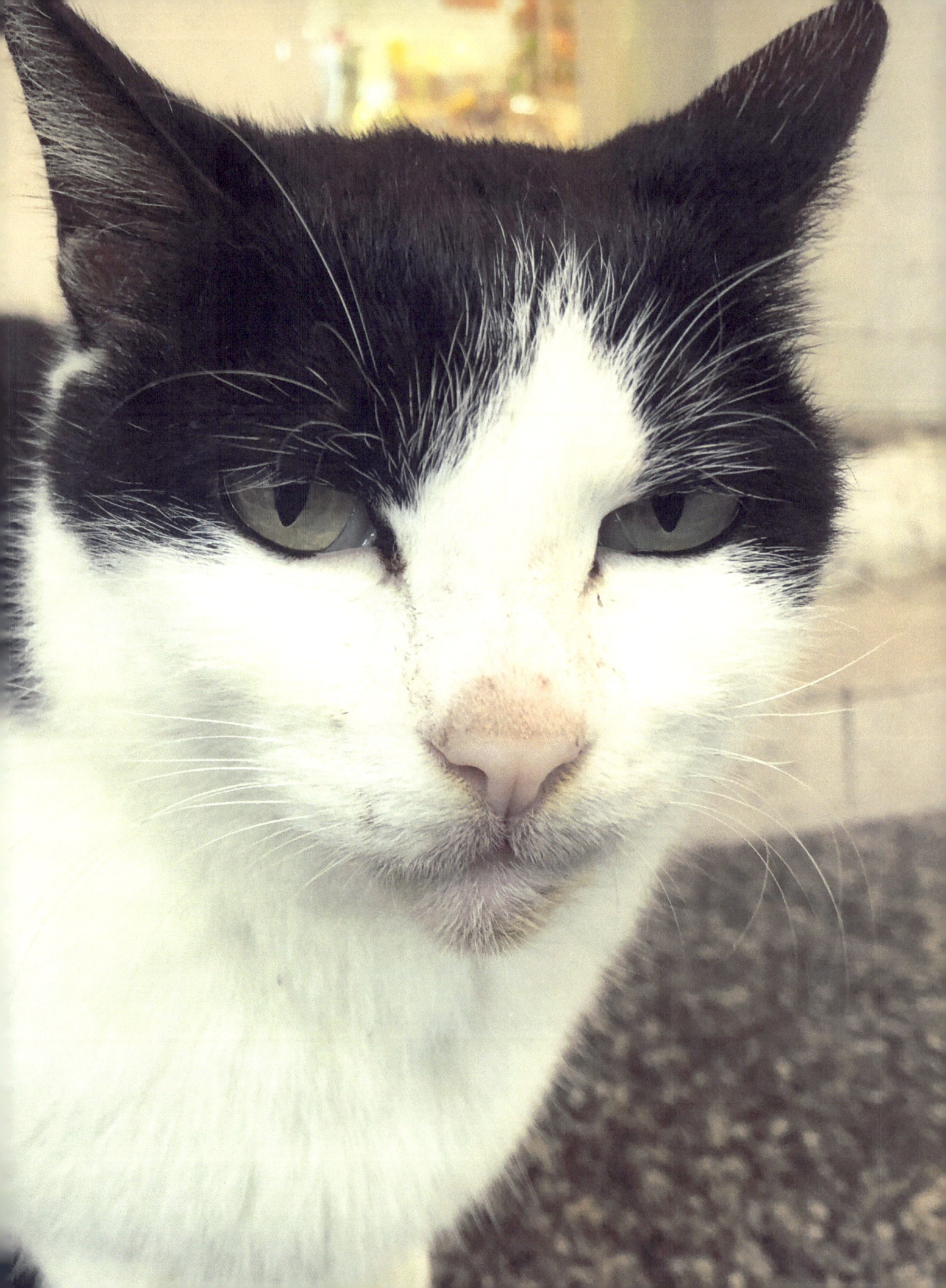

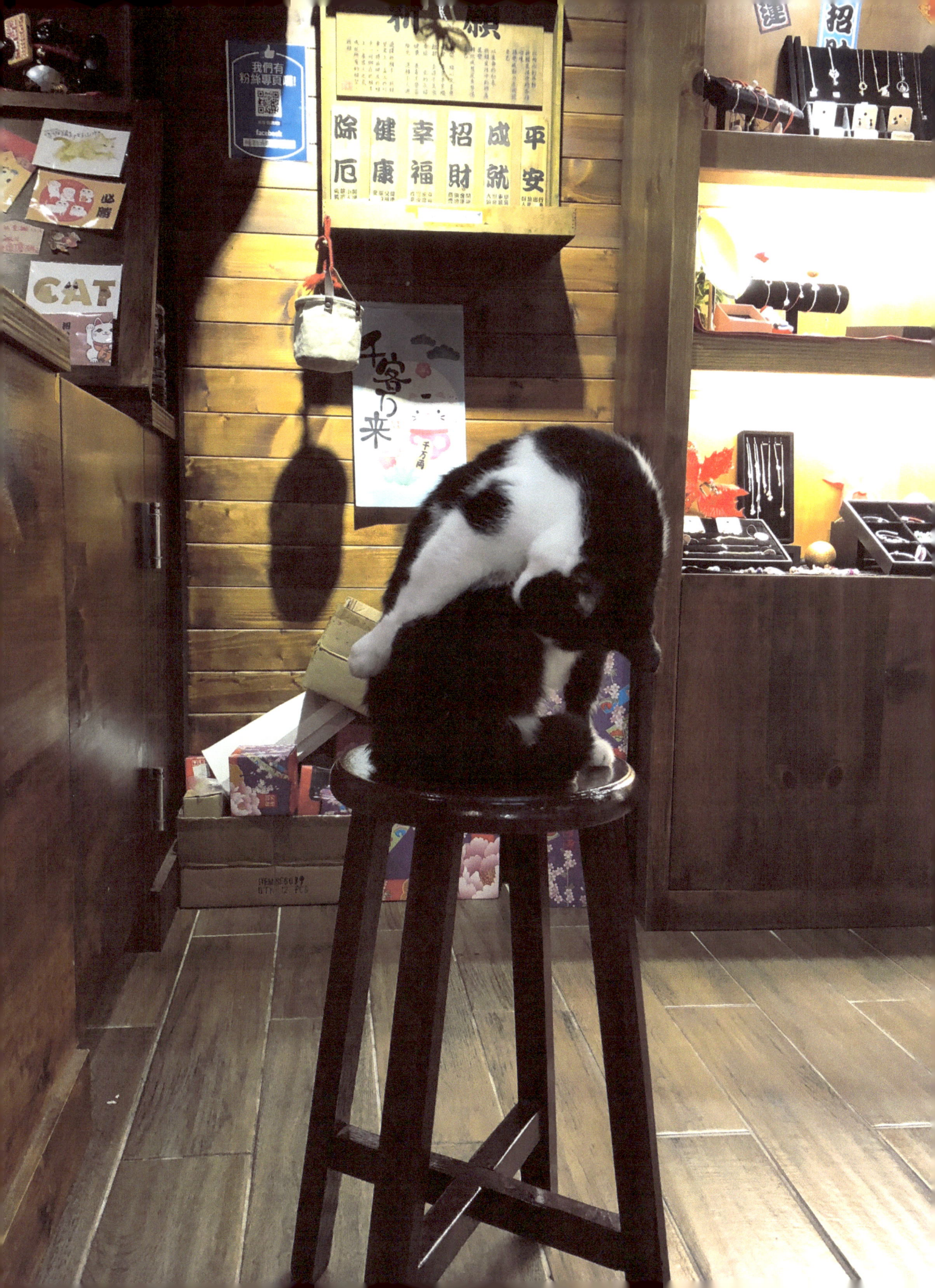

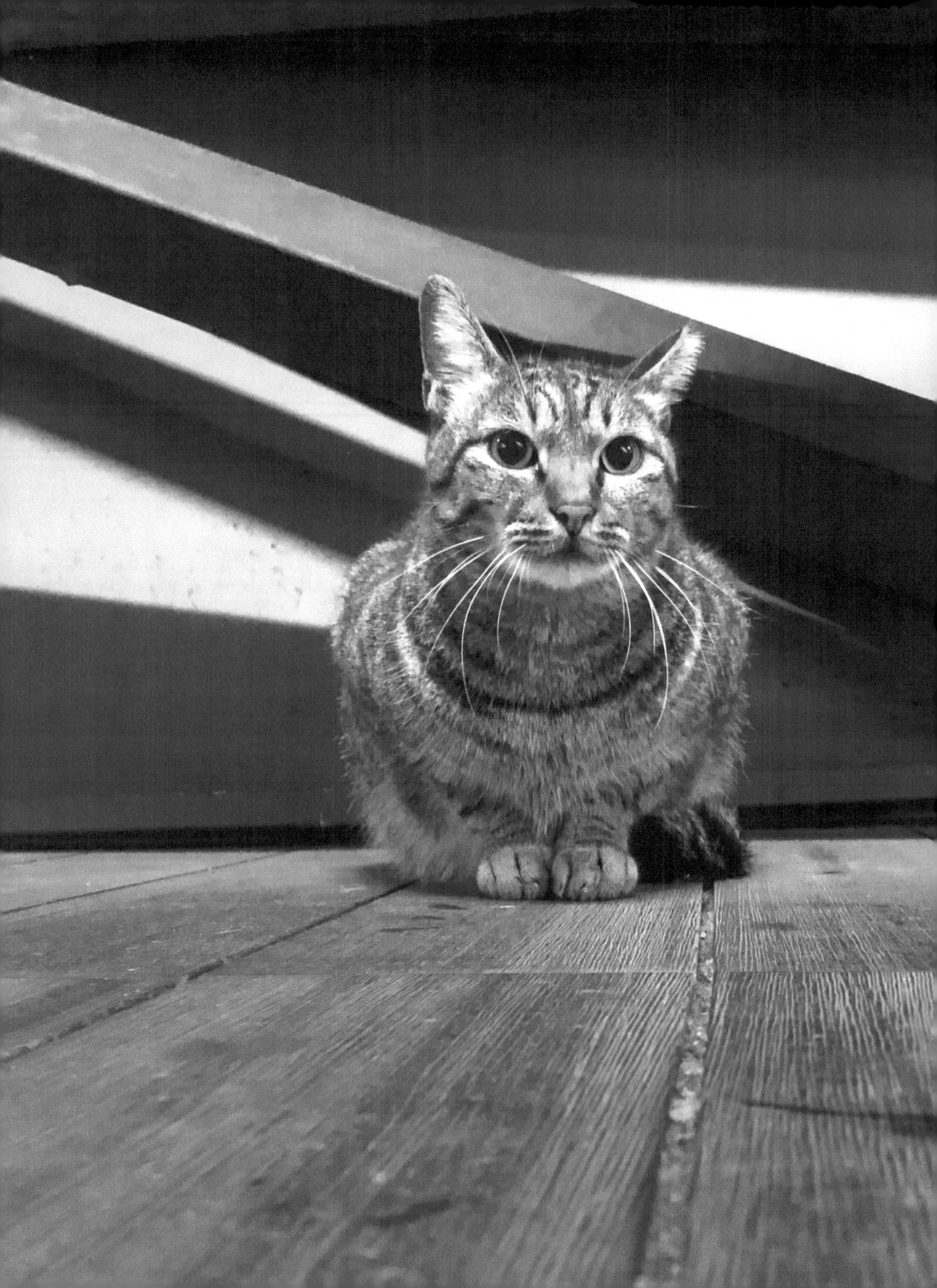

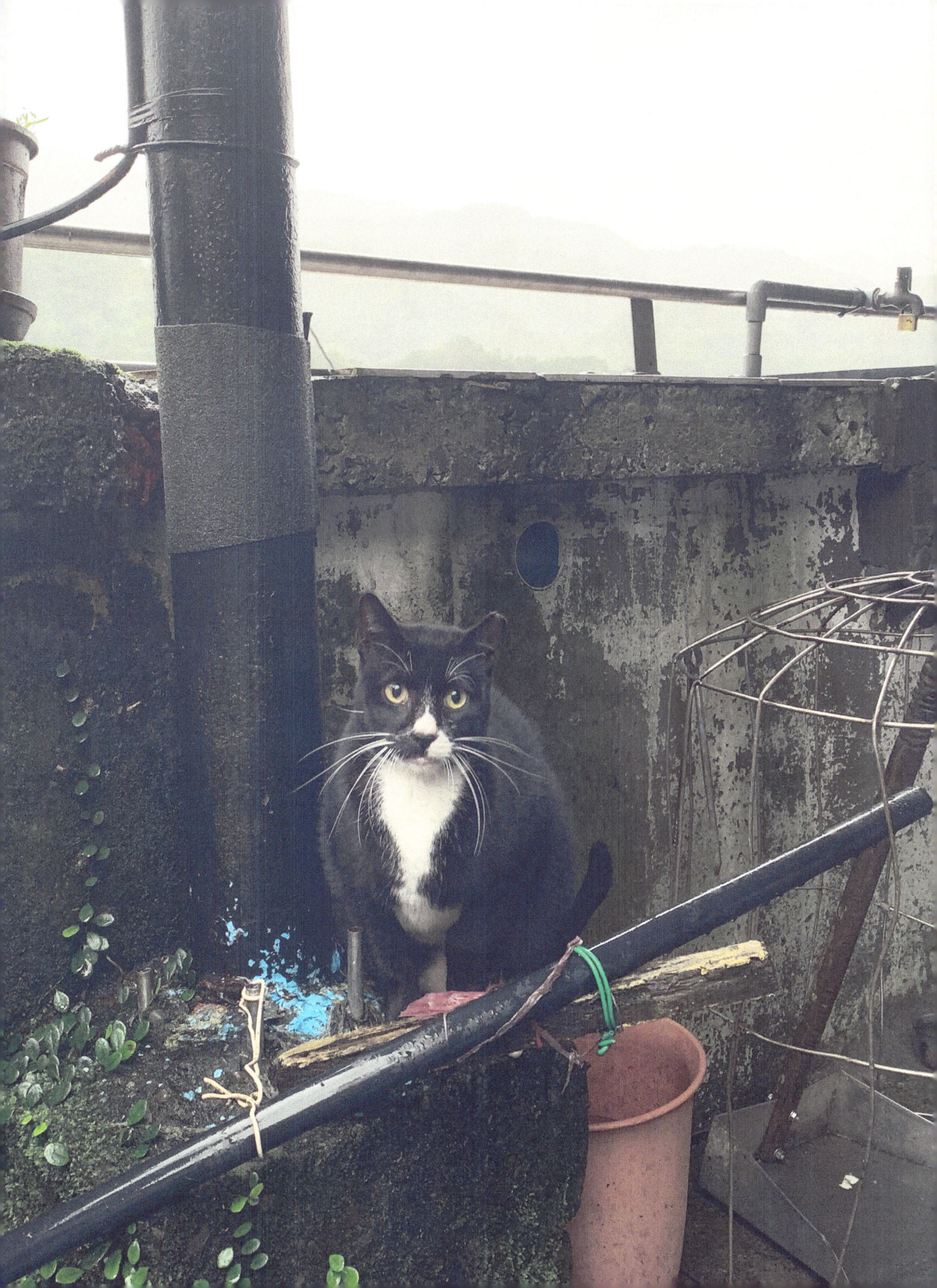

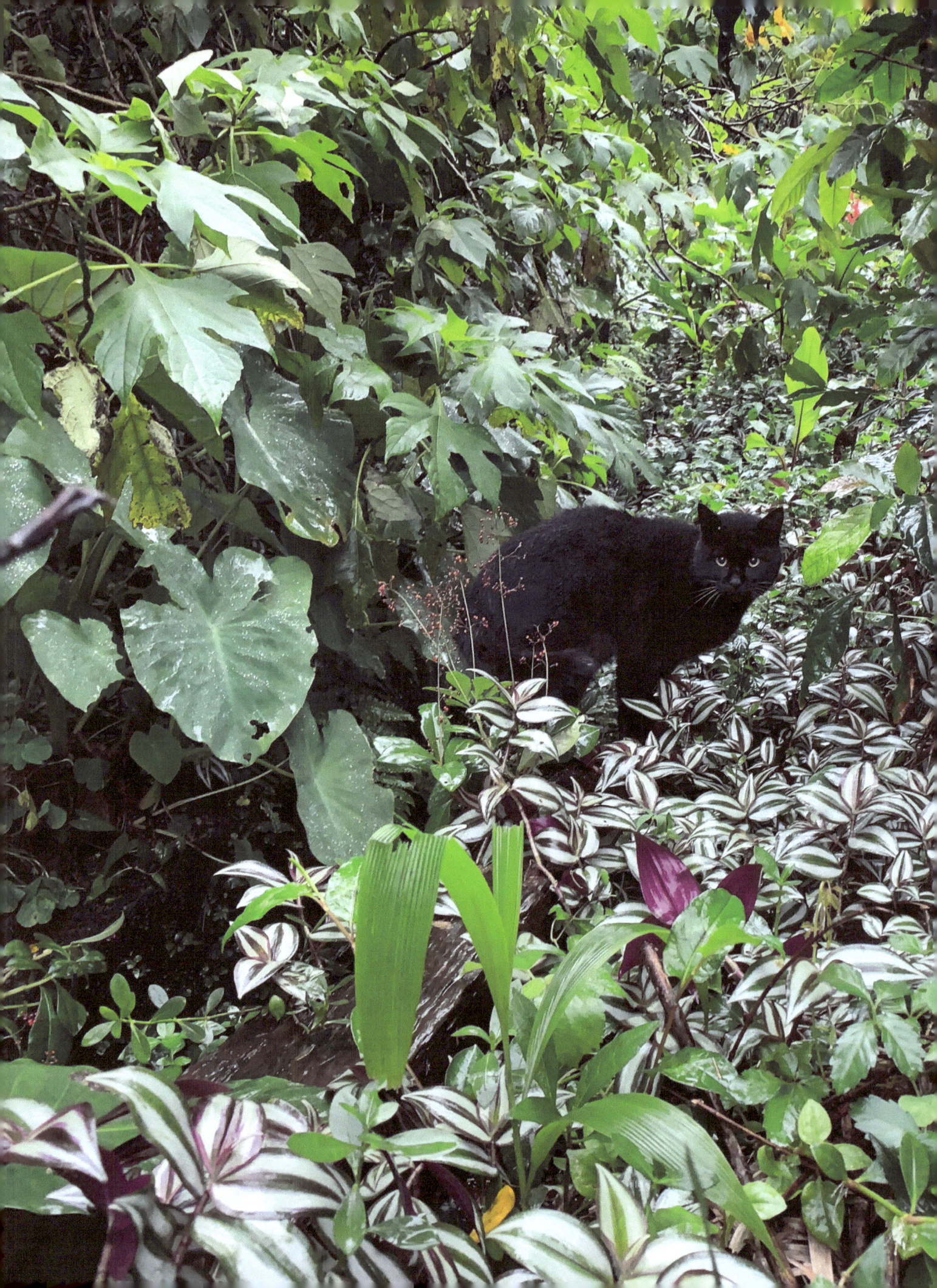

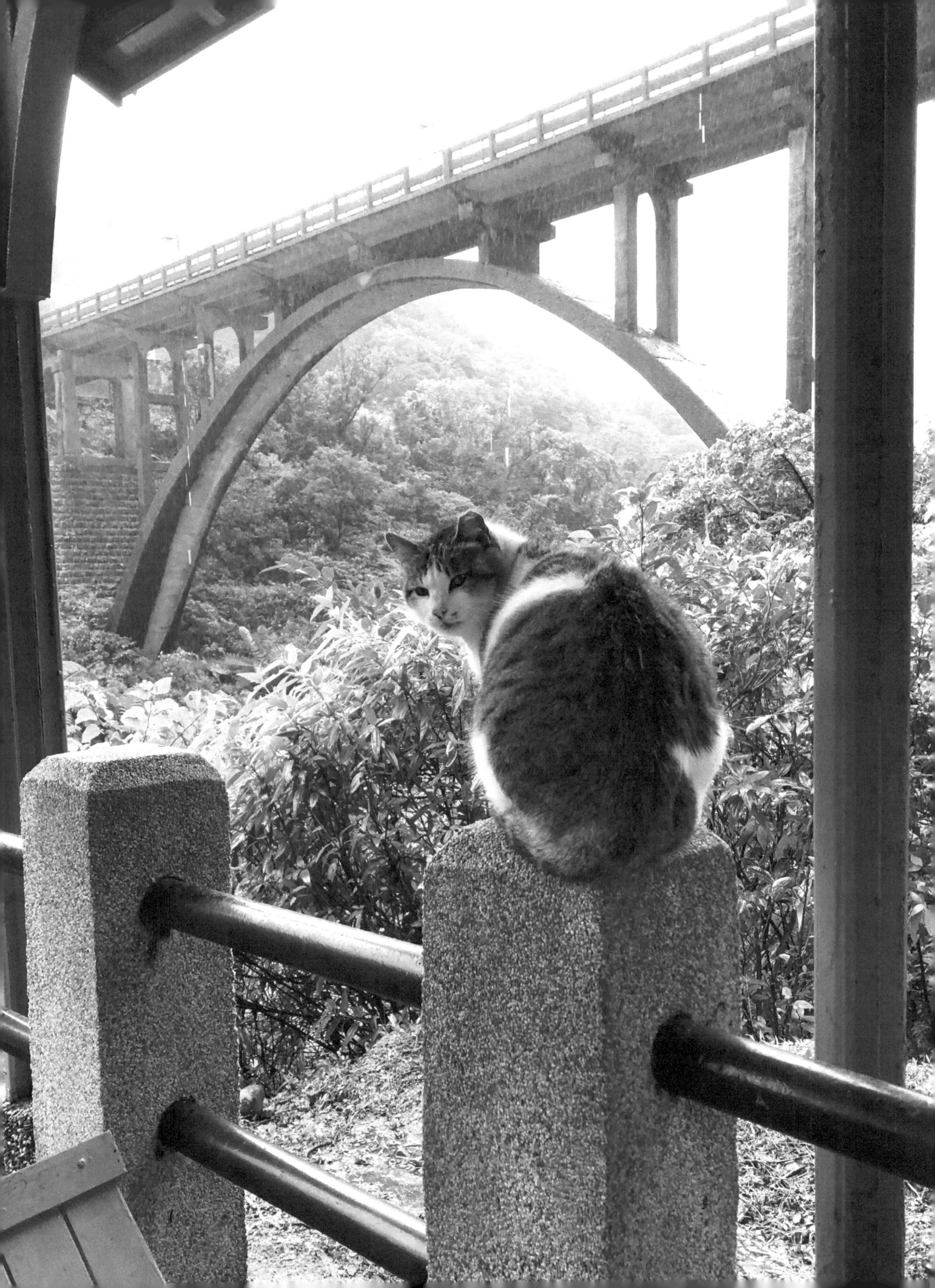

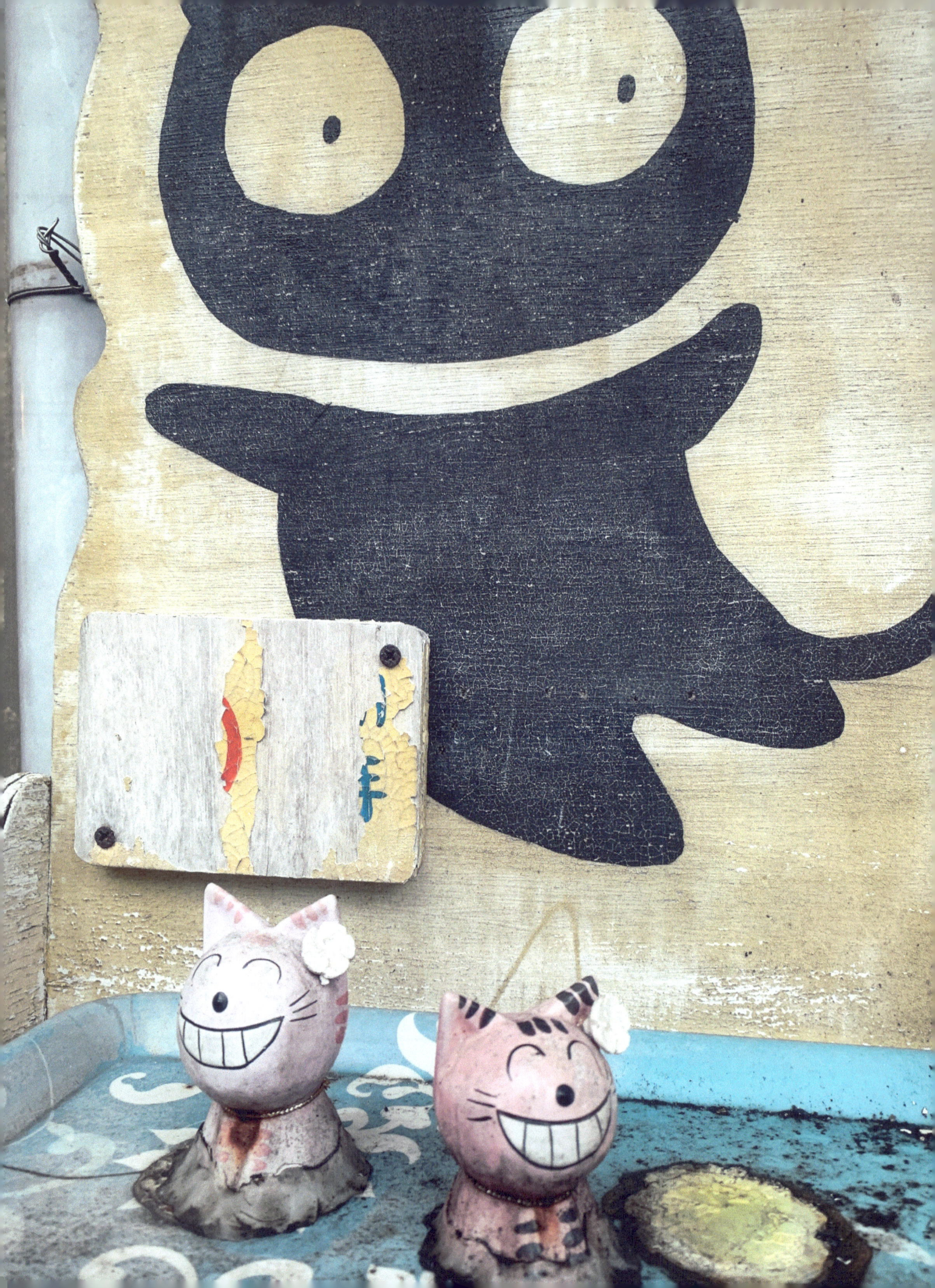

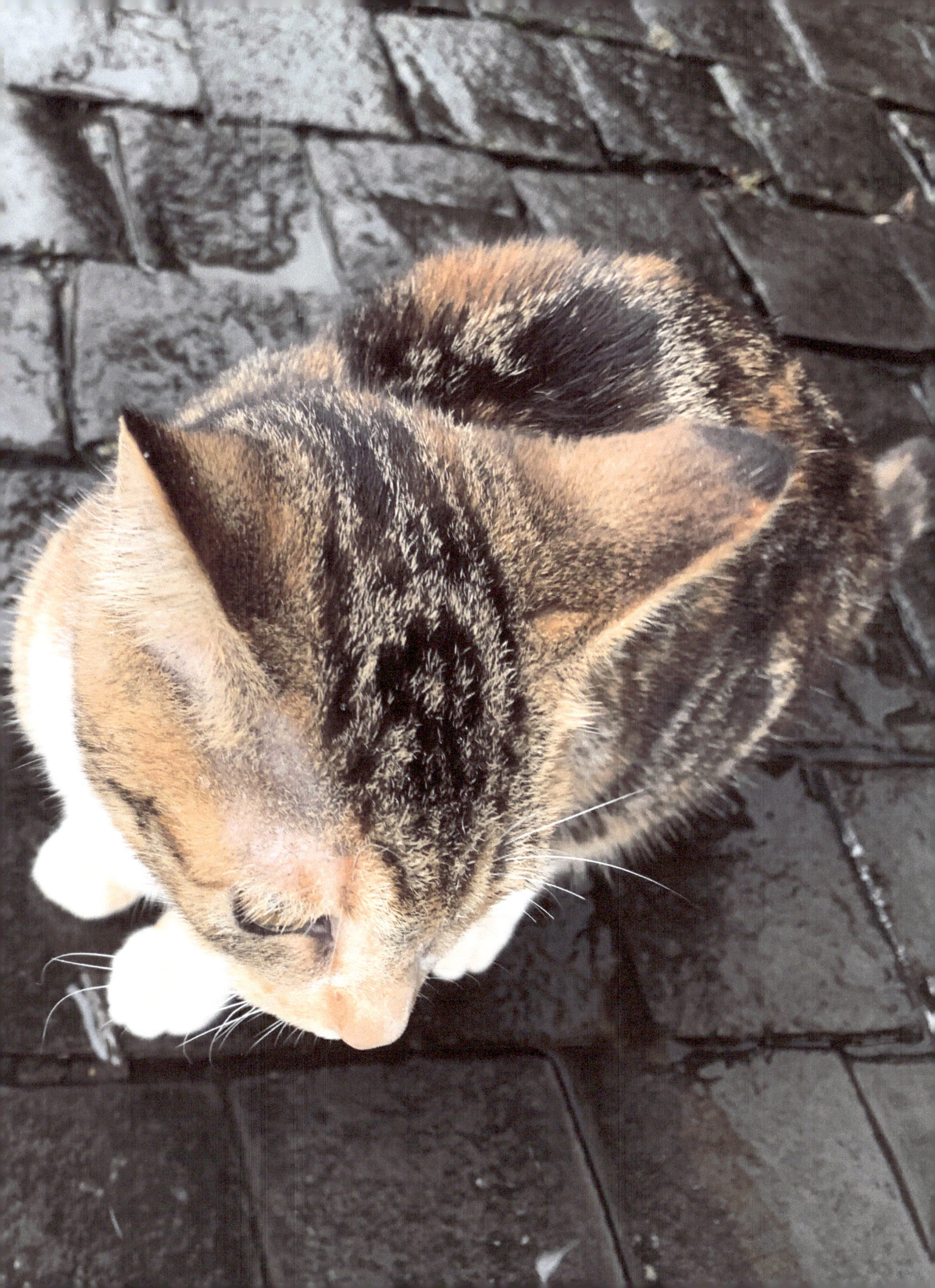

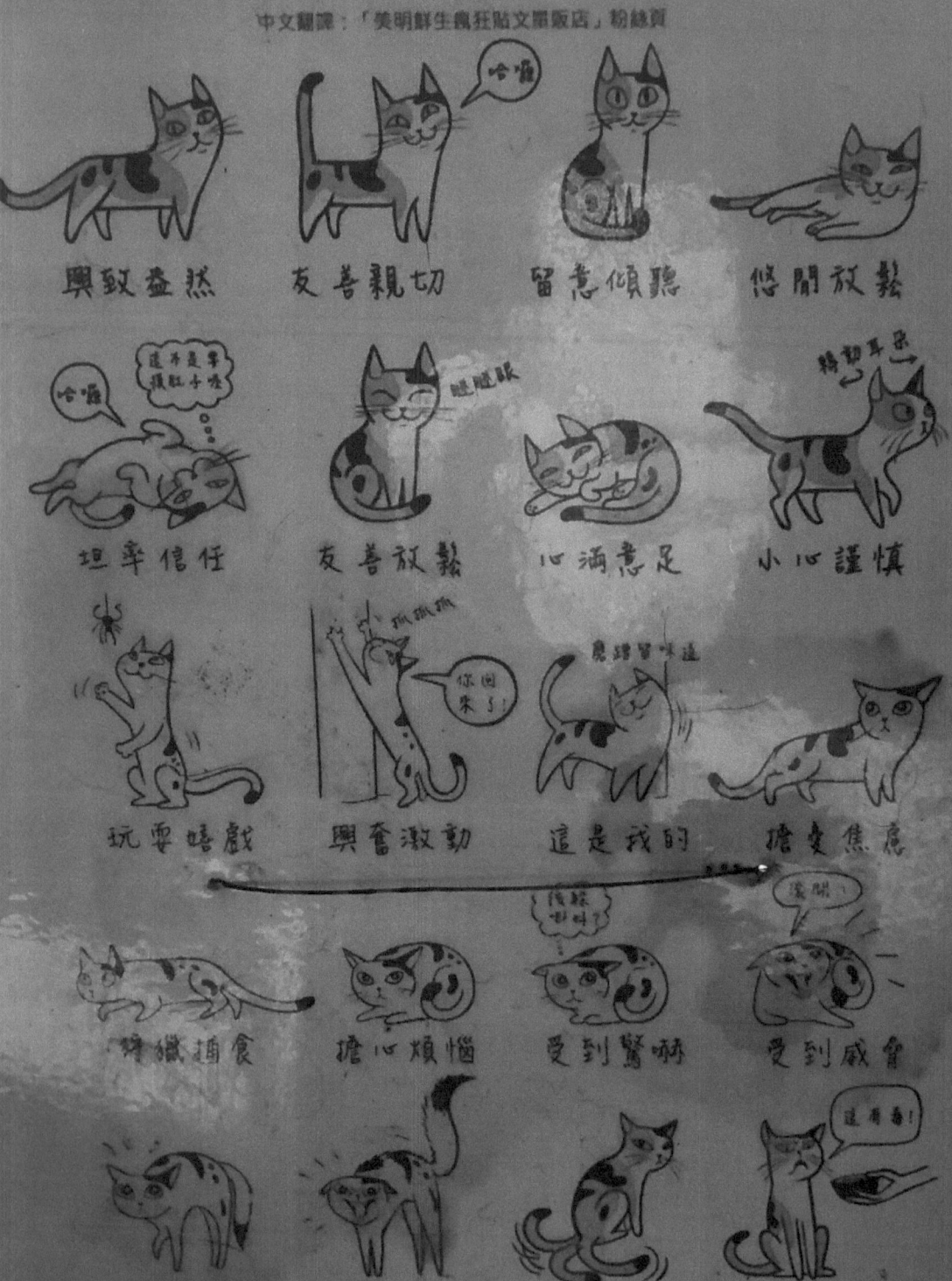

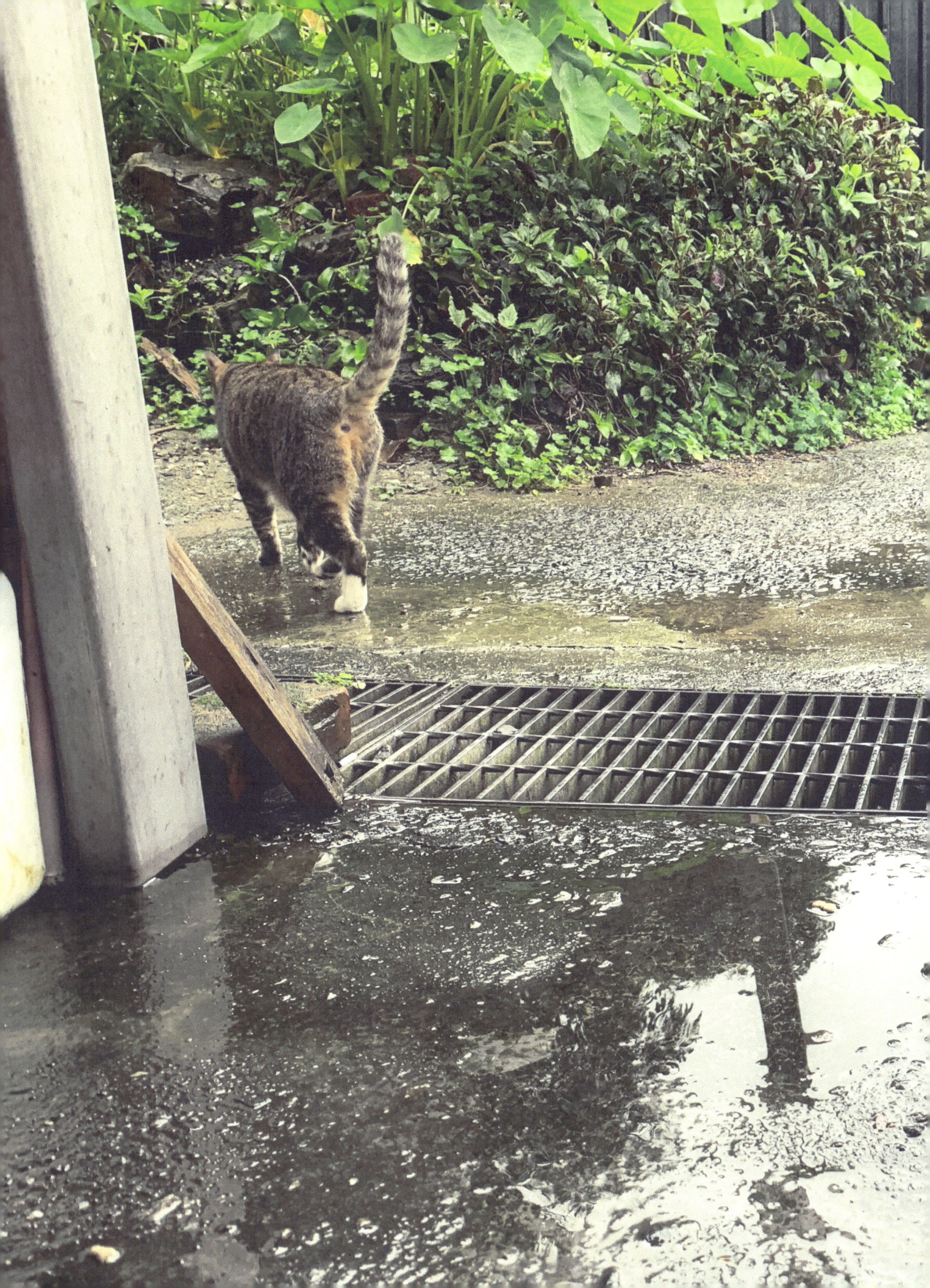

www.ingramcontent.com/pod-product-compliance
Lightning Source LLC
Chambersburg PA
CBHW051220220526
45473CB00003B/1110